HOW TO MAKE A KILLING IN THE

ALTERNATIVE INVESTMENT MARKET

by

Michael Walters

First published 1995
This edition (3rd impression) 1997

© Michael Walters

British Library Cataloguing in Publication Data. A catalogue record for this book is available from the British Library.

ISBN 0 948035 23 4

Cover Design by Peter Higgins
Book Design by MacWing

Published by:
Rushmere Wynne Group PLC
4-5 Harmill, Grovebury Road,
Leighton Buzzard
Bedfordshire LU7 8FF
Tel: 01525 853726
Fax: 01525 852037

Printed by:
Redwood Books Limited
Kennet House, Kennet Way
Trowbridge, Wiltshire B14 8RN

HOW TO MAKE A KILLING IN THE
ALTERNATIVE INVESTMENT MARKET

by

Michael Walters

Rushmere Wynne Limited
England

Other books by Michael Walters

How To Make A Killing In Penny Shares
How To Make A Killing In The Share Jungle
How To Make A Killing In New Issues
How To Profit From Your Personal Equity Plan
How To Profit From The Coming Share Boom

DO NOT READ THIS BOOK

◆ If you do not understand that the stockmarket is a dangerous place where you can lose all of the money you have put into it.

◆ If you do not want to gamble in one of the riskiest sectors of the stockmarket.

◆ If you are content to leave the biggest stockmarket winners to others, and to miss an awful lot of fun.

CONTENTS

INTRODUCTION

Welcome to the wilder side of the great share game, where the risks are rougher and the rewards richer. Please read no further if you are interested in the stockmarket as a place where you can buy shares for long-term protection against inflation — a livelier alternative to the building society or the bank deposit account. There is nothing wrong with that. It makes good sense. It is just that this is not the book for you, and the fledgling markets are no place for you or your money.

The Alternative Investment Market, or its wilder cousin, the OFEX market, are among the riskiest areas of stockmarket investment — though they are certainly not the most lethal. There are more dangerous share games you can play, and which I would advise you to avoid unless you have constant expert advice. The traded-options market offers more lethal opportunities for losing all of your money — and more — more rapidly. And in my view, anyone who plays in small Australian and Irish stocks wants his head examined — or, at least, his wallet removed. But then that will probably happen pretty quickly regardless.

You should also be clear that this Alternative Investment Market has nothing to do with dabbling in antiques, stamps, teddy bears, and any other old tosh. That, to my mind, is really speculative investment, much of it in markets where it is all too easy to buy, and well-nigh impossible to sell at anything like the price you paid. Such markets make the whole of the Stock Exchange look positively staid and rock-solid by comparison. Stay away.

It might not be easy, but for anyone who goes in with his eyes open, the stockmarket version of the Alternative Investment Market offers some of the most exciting opportunities anywhere. So long as the stockmarket proper and the economy are in reasonable shape, the risks are not unreasonable when set against the potential rewards. Make no mistake, though. If the main market is in free fall, and the economy is heading for trouble, the AIM and the OFEX are not the places to be.

No one knows how these fledgling markets for fledgling companies will fare if total gloom envelops the Stock Exchange proper. As I write, that has not been tested. But a falling market could mean mayhem if you are there when it happens — though hopefully you will have heeded the advice in this book and taken your leave and your cash in good time. In the mid-nineties, there are certainly grounds for hope that we might see several years of economic progress, which would lay the foundations for a solid and sustainable market developing on the AIM and further excitement on the OFEX. No guarantees, though.

This book is full of wealth warnings. I mean every single one. But for those who are ready to gamble with money they can afford to lose, the AIM is the opportunity market, where the private investor might punt a few hundred pounds and end up with several thousand inside a year or two. Or a few thousand pounds might just be transformed into tens of thousands. With luck. And with nerve.

When I wrote the first edition of this book late in 1994, it might have seemed extraordinary to make such claims. I was writing before the AIM officially began in June 1995. Happily, even in the first year of AIM trading, it did prove possible to make a killing, if you were swift, brave, and lucky enough.

Successful investment is all about anticipation. Exciting signs were plain to see in the AIM and OFEX market, even in their first year. Nurtured by pioneers such as John Jenkins, Brian Winterflood, and the enterprising corporate finance departments of many medium and smaller stockbrokers, some innovative companies seized the chance to float shares and raise money to build their business. It quickly became possible to buy or sell the shares in several such companies, freely and in reasonable quantities, with competing quotations. And there were some terrific early winners, with remarkably few significant losers.

As the AIM becomes established, there are many more smaller companies planning to use it to raise money. Furious at the way they were treated by the banks in the recession of the early nineties, unhappy that borrowings can be called in at short notice, despairing at the lack of vision which forces bank managers to reject any but the most copper-bottomed business plans, and determined not put their homes and the future of their families on the line with personal guarantees, small company promoters are beginning to see that the AIM and perhaps the OFEX have tossed them a life-line. They can raise outside risk capital without giving away control of their company, and without surrendering a fortune to greedy venture capitalists who want to tell them how they should run their businesses.

Already, within a year of being launched, the AIM is tapping into a reservoir of management talent eager to succeed with the support of adventurous investors who are ready to take a risk in the hope of higher returns.

There are surveys galore suggesting that backing small companies generates a return much superior to that from sticking with the big boys, risks and all. There will be more as the City continues to wake up to the potential of the AIM, and devises more products to tap into it. There are successful investment trusts devoted to AIM already. They know that the more attention the City pays, the more the market will prosper.

In November 1994, the Gartmore unit trust giant commissioned a new index from Professors Elroy Dimson and Paul Marsh of the London Business School, designed to track the bottom one per cent of the UK equity market by value of company. Well known for their work in establishing the superior performance of smaller companies, Dimson and Marsh tracked back to 1955. If their MicroCap Index had been in existence then, it would have generated an annualised total return of 22%, against 14.5% for the FT-SE All Share index, even after taking into account the collapse of some of the small companies.

Many other surveys confirm the trend. Small companies grow more quickly than large ones. And if you spread the risk sufficiently to offset the impact of a few total losses among the tiddlers, your investment need not be much more exposed to the downside. Not, of course, that big boys are immune from collapse. Do I hear Brent Walker, Maxwell Communications Corporation, and my old friend Polly Peck?

Anyone checking new issues on the main market from late 1993 to late 1994 would be forced to conclude that backing big names is hardly the way to a killing. Companies large and small left investors cursing as they fell short of their forecasts, and their share prices plunged. They were sponsored by some of the most revered names in the City, from Warburg to Rothschild to Lazards and Robert Fleming.

There were far fewer problems among the tiddlers, new names appearing for the first time on the AIM. Perhaps the difficulties are yet to come. Perhaps not.

As AIM moves ahead, it is being supported by acres of press comment. But it is still relatively unknown, shunned by many major investment houses, with share prices listed in relatively few papers. And if some think the AIM is obscure, hardly anyone seems to know about the OFEX, or understand it. In investment, those who spot the opportunities first gain the biggest pickings. Hopefully, this book will help readers to win an extra advantage by getting aboard early.

There may be much to be gained. Later in this book, I discuss Tracker Network, a company with a device for recovering stolen cars. Tracker shares were launched at 257p on the 4.2 market, the market which preceded the AIM and the OFEX. Within a year, Tracker was trading at more than £15. Original subscribers multiplied their money six-fold very swiftly, though the shares later slipped back to around 600p. You may have heard of the device, but probably never realised the shares were alive and trading busily, first on the 4.2 market, then on AIM.

IES Group, an electronic security systems company, was launched at the equivalent of less than 9p in December 1993. By the spring of 1996, having developed contracts with British Airways and assorted High Street big names, plus a system for recording on disk the identity of cash machine users, the shares were trading on the OFEX at more than 300p. Early investors multiplied their money more than 30-fold, if you include the benefit of warrants given away in the issue.

Biotechnology specialist Scotia Holdings was another which performed brilliantly on the 4.2 market before making its debut on the full Exchange. Initially it proved a touch disappointing, but those who spotted it early on the 4.2 market will have no regrets. By the summer of 1996, Scotia was forging ahead, trading at almost three times the Stock Exchange opening price.

> "Early investors on the AIM multiplied their money more than 30-fold"

Exceptional? Obviously. But three such super winners from the limited early list is a pretty remarkable proportion. It ignores the odd exotic oil play which has scored phenomenal share gains, despite my abhorrence of such companies. And it does not cover some of the exciting issues popping up in 1996.

In just the first 12 months of trading on AIM, there were winners enough to satisfy almost anyone. Financial Publications leapt nearly seven-fold, from 38p to 260p. Pan Andean Resources multiplied five-fold from 18p to 90p. ViewInn, a media business, went from 100p to 615p, restaurant company Ask Central from 35p to 133p.

OFEX is not quite so easy to track, but the first nine months saw some remarkable performances. Syence Skin Care moved between 9.5p and 66p, Proginet from 20p to 55p, while Motion Media multiplied four-fold. SkyNet rocketed to 10 times the issue price, before being suspended in a blaze of controversy. Make no mistake, these are all high-risk issues. By the time you read this, the picture might have changed dramatically — for better or worse. Use the sort of selling sense rules which are explained in Chapter Ten, however, and you might manage to capture most of the upside without too much of the pain.

As yet, the market is young, but already the big winners way outnumber the big losers among companies which made their debut from 1993 onwards. It would be wrong to suggest that any of the individual shares mentioned in this book will go on to make a fortune — this is not a tip sheet — but some might. And there are other intriguing companies which might catch the imagination of the small share speculator.

Some of them set my mouth watering. But I am a speculator by nature. My personal investment resources are modest. Twice I have made fairly large amounts from playing the market. One lot I lost entirely in the 1974 crash. The second took a battering in the October 1987 crash, though I spent a good chunk of my profits before the fall, and did not lose all my money. Because I have limited capital, I often play in high-risk, high-return situations. A 10% or 20% gain is no good on small amounts. You want double — or better — or quits. This high-risk approach has brought me some spectacular gains. Perhaps I might do it again, in the AIM and OFEX area. For the record, I have invested in several such companies. Most have done well for me. Some are mentioned in this book, and include one monster winner, IES Group.

My original IES investment was more a result of good fortune and a good stockbroker than my investment skill, though I have increased my stake along the way. I mention it to satisfy those who, reasonably enough, ask that if the author is smart enough to give investment advice, why hasn't he made a killing himself?

Here and there, I have. And there is evidence of my strengths and weaknesses on display regularly in the *Daily Mail*. In the mid-eighties, I ran a highly successful share tipping column, the only one which suggested when to sell as well as when to buy. I gave up in the middle of 1986, fearful that the market was too high. My timing was a year early.

Since October 1992, I have been running a fairly regular tipping column in the *Mail*. When the *Mail* Monday City page was abolished in the spring of 1996, I am delighted to say that many readers wrote to the editor to complain. As a result, the column was restored, but on Saturdays. That is perhaps the most telling testimony to its success, better than my own boasts. It has done well, with a few spectacular successes, and has recommended a smattering of AIM stocks. Again, it is the only column which follows its own bad tips as well as the good, and monitors every tip until there is a recommendation to sell. That, I believe, is the only responsible way.

I mention my tipping columns to make the point that this book is no warmed-up meal of cold investment theories. For better or for worse, I have been playing the share market for 30 years, sometimes winning, sometimes being badly bruised. Many of my investment ideas are there in print for all to see, week in and week out. I know what it feels like to lose money in the stock-market. And to make it. You can get some insight into my progress by watching the *Mail*, seeing how it goes, as it happens. I would never dream of recommending a stock to readers which I was not prepared to buy myself.

That matters. Make up your own mind about investment writers who tell you they never trade in shares as a matter of principle. The theory and the practice of investment are very different. I have written several books on investment. They lack the depth of theory some authors can bring to bear (Jim Slater is far and away the best in conveying it in practical, comprehensible fashion, though Bob Beckman has an unrivalled command of more theories than you could ever imagine existed). My efforts reflect the benefits of over 30 years writing about the City in simple language, stumbling about with money of my own in the share market, and watching and talking to a few investment superstars, and an awful lot of crooks and conmen.

Above all, I hope they show a passionate belief as a financial journalist and investment author that it is worth trying to even up the odds, to try to help the private investor compete in a game where the professional has enormous advantages — and sometimes a few disadvantages.

The AIM and the OFEX are high-risk markets. They are not for everyone. The crooks and conmen are already pushing in around the edges. But because they are starting too small to attract the big money boys, they offer special opportunities for the private punter, the small investor who is prepared to take a gamble — and the small company promoter with ambitious ideas. I would never have written this book without being convinced that it can serve a valuable purpose for private investors, helping them through the jungle, dodging some of the traps, spotting some of the very real rewards which are there, if only you can find them.

And it should be fun. Never let it get too serious. Please only use money you can afford to lose. Heed my warnings and try to spread your risk over three or four different companies. Good luck.

Michael Walters
London
September 1996.

1

What Is The Alternative Investment Market?

The Alternative Investment Market is the most risky share market anywhere under the wing of the London Stock Exchange. Get that straight. Conventional investment folk will warn you off it, if they know how it works — and even if they do not. If you get irritated by the repeated warnings in this book about the speculative nature of the AIM, so much the better. That means the message is getting through. It means you understand the dangers.

It is not all bad. Far from it. The AIM is the opportunity market, the place where you can make a killing. And the market where unique tax perks are really something rather special. They help to redress the balance a little when you play the high-risk, high-reward gambling table, the place where you can make a real killing.

You can spot a small and ambitious company and see your investment grow as the company grows. Get it right, and the satisfaction of being in something exciting at the beginning will be multiplied by the more tangible reward of making a very handsome capital gain. Get it right, and your shares will not simply grow in line with the company, but will rise more quickly as the word spreads, and as the rating of that company grows.

Get it wrong, and you could lose the lot. No appeal, no argument. A total loss, pure and simple. Unless, of course, you spot the decline coming, and sell on the way down. We have ways of helping you to do that. Perhaps the most important chapter in this book is Chapter Ten, which tells you about selling. Heed it, and perhaps you will never suffer a total loss — though you are almost certain to lose money on some of the shares in the AIM, no matter how careful you may be.

Any responsible account is duty bound to emphasise the extremes. The reality may be less dramatic. In the first year, not one AIM company went bust, while perhaps a dozen or more doubled in value — or better.

The most spectacular example of the pluses and minuses was that of Memory Corporation, which had a system for using defective computer memory chips. It soared from under 20p to 555p in the first few months of dealing, hit problems, and tumbled to 50p. Plenty of room there to make big money, and to lose it. A similar story applies to Firecrest, a marketing company which announced a series of ventures linked to the Internet. That roared from 38p to 203p, then back down to 31p. SCS Satellite was another sorry disappointment, hitting 133p, and dropping to 31p before being suspended with major problems. But the big winners significantly outnumbered the heavy losers. South American oil explorer Pan Andean Resources raced from 18p to top 90p. Stanford Rook, which may have a compound to tackle TB, rocketed from 100p to touch 600p.

How It Started

The Alternative Investment Market started as a Stock Exchange initiative to encourage investment in small companies, to offer them a cheaper, easier way of raising money, and perhaps to attract investors in their locality. That, at least, is something like the official line. Many sceptics see it differently. They believe the Exchange was threatened by plans to set up markets for shares in smaller companies outside the Exchange, and cobbled together the AIM in order to preserve a monopoly of share markets in the UK. Take your pick.

The Exchange had attempted previously to set up markets in smaller company shares. In the seventies, it was criticised by a committee headed by the then Harold Wilson for failing to provide finance for small companies. In 1978, it allowed limited trading in unquoted shares under a special rule 163 (4) for matching buyers and sellers. In November 1980, it got altogether more serious, launching the Unlisted Securities Market, a cheaper and more flexible version of the fully listed market. Companies were allowed aboard with a shorter trading record, and the proprietors could keep a larger proportion of their shares.

Inevitably, the USM succumbed to creeping red tape and professional greed, and the cost of floating companies on it crept higher and closer to the cost of a full listing. In the mid-eighties, a series of companies licensed by the Department of Trade to conduct investment business moved from the telephone selling of shares on the official markets to floating companies of their own. The Over-The-Counter market was born, with Harvard Securities, Ravendale and Afcor among the more notorious names.

They are not with us now. They all collapsed in an unhappy heap, leaving investors with trading losses and often with shares in companies which went bust, or simply drifted away. A few of the OTC flotation companies did thrive. Not all were duds and some made it to a full listing, while others were taken over by large quoted companies. The Hard Rock Café chain started on the OTC. So did Tadpole Technology and Applied Holographics.

By and large, the OTC investment houses relied on the aggressive telephone promotion of shares in companies they had floated. When the OTC empire collapsed, the market in the shares disappeared. But while the game lasted, it proved a serious threat to the Stock Exchange monopoly. It did raise some money for small businesses, and the salesmen filled a need among small investors for personal advice. Sadly, when the going got tough, the need to sell shares overtook the notion of serving investors, and it became a scramble to earn commission at any price.

The Stock Exchange responded to the OTC by launching the Third Market. This was intended to allow small companies to gain a listing of sorts cheaply, with light regulation. It never really got off the ground, and was effectively killed by the stockmarket crash of October 1987. Shares in Third Market companies became very difficult to buy or sell, and the market was finally formally killed in 1991.

Rule 4.2

Alongside this, the Exchange expanded the rule allowing the intermittent trading of shares on a matched bargain basis, replacing rule 163 (4) by rule 535.2. That developed into rule 4.2, and became much more flexible, with the Exchange granting permission for trading in specific shares for 12 months at a time, instead of requiring to approve each individual bargain.

That began to attract more attention, helped significantly by market-maker J.P. Jenkins setting up a book in many stocks, agreeing to buy and sell at prices in set quantities regularly displayed on the screens available in broking offices. From a market where buyers and sellers were matched, the rule 4.2 market became the equivalent to a junior listed market in the shares of many companies.

Throughout 1994, the 4.2 market grew much more active, and more than 30 companies used it to raise about £60m. A list of broking houses ready to sponsor such issues began to evolve, and active markets developed in the shares of several companies. At least one — formerly the Wilton Group, but now called Pacific Media — stepped down from the USM to the 4.2 market.

This formed the basis for what became the AIM in the summer of 1995. The official launch attracted much more attention to such companies, raising their ratings. In less than a year, there were more than 160 companies on the AIM. It had developed into a serious market for serious money, even though many of the stuffier City houses still tended to stay away.

OFEX

As AIM took off, the Rule 4.2 market faded out, to be replaced by an impressive new initiative from Rule 4.2 experts J.P. Jenkins. Not all the 4.2 companies wanted to go on to AIM. Some were too small, some too shy. So John Jenkins created an Off Exchange Market to allow shares in such companies to be traded. A few giants settled there. Top of the lot in size is National Parking Corporation, which in November 1994 called off talks which might have brought a bid valuing the company at more than £700m. Food group Weetabix, with a market value of more than £300m, also opted for OFEX.

Such companies are exceptional, however. In the main, the OFEX market has developed into a low-cost, junior market for companies at the very beginning of the scale. Jenkins charges just a few thousand pounds a year to list companies, and to carry details of their activities on the Newstrack service. This shows buying and selling prices, and records recent trades in the shares, and appears on TV screens all around the City. It also carries pages showing recent announcements, and others recording the basic financial details of all OFEX traded companies. As a handy reference, it is first class, superior in some ways to the facilities available for AIM companies. There is also a regular monthly Newstrack magazine, carrying details of OFEX companies. Called *OFX*, it is published by Newstrack Ltd, Moor House, 119 London Wall, London EC2Y 5ET, and is available by subscription.

Jenkins vets companies coming to OFEX. He has a committee which checks the particulars, and it works reasonably well. Be under no illusion, however. OFEX offers some fascinating opportunities, and there have been some big share winners, with prices which have multiplied three- or four-fold in a year. It is a high-risk, speculative market. But there really are times when it is not possible to buy or sell some of the securities listed on OFEX for months on end. You could buy one day, and find you cannot sell for months, while the price plunges out of sight. In the first year of trading, there have been no disasters, no total collapses. But there could be. And you could have a lost a lot of money if you got it wrong. OFEX is very much the junior, wilder cousin to the AIM — and some people consider AIM too risky. Most of the comments in this book about dealing in AIM also apply to OFEX, but with the warnings writ larger and clearer. If you think twice about playing on AIM — and you should — think 10 times about trading on OFEX.

The AIM Outline

Happily, the Stock Exchange has taken a relaxed approach to inviting discussion over the rules for AIM. It does mean, however, that company vetting and reporting standards are not as high as for those listed on the main market.

It is possible to float on AIM with a prospectus which is prepared by a sponsor who is not a member of the Stock Exchange. Some accounting firms have sponsored issues, and other specialists, such as Neill Clerk Capital, have also been busy in the AIM game. Initial fears that a two-tier market might develop,

"If you think twice about playing on AIM — think 10 times about trading on OFEX"

with companies sponsored by Stock Exchange member firms attracting a higher investment rating, have proved unfounded. Some investors, though, may prefer companies which make it clear from the beginning that they intend to graduate as soon as they can to a full Stock Exchange listing. Such companies will be eager to ensure that they conform as closely as possible to the rules of the full market, without committing themselves to the full expense.

The Stock Exchange does not vet AIM flotation documents, so they must be approached with extra care. Inevitably, they involve additional risk, no matter how carefully they appear to be presented.

Investors are not left in the dark, however. AIM prospectuses do carry the kind of historic profits information, where it exists, as any flotation document. They should have all of the information that any investor would normally require to form a reasonable view. Significantly, that includes details of all directors' previous directorships going back five years. Directors have to abide by the same dealing code as listed companies — no insider dealing — but may have more leeway on reporting deals with related companies.

The idea is not to encumber new companies with so many obligations that raising money on the AIM becomes too expensive. It is intended to be a cheap and easy way of gaining access to funds, though even within the first year, that good intention has been eroded by what seems an inevitable trend towards extra red tape and higher costs. All being well, local markets for local companies will develop. The Scots seem especially keen on this. A variety of other interesting initiatives have been debated. It remains to see how many translate into reality.

The Tax Advantages

Though many investors have been slow to appreciate it, there is a growing awareness that AIM and OFEX companies come with important tax advantages. In some cases, these are sufficient to encourage companies to remain on AIM. And there is a real prospect that they will eventually generate a premium in some AIM shares because they are so valuable. Many market professionals who scored substantial capital gains on the main market in 1995 have been paying extra attention to the AIM as a way of trimming tax bills.

Inheritance Tax Relief

Some AIM or OFEX flotations have been managed partly to take advantage of inheritance tax relief. This is available for shares in unquoted companies, and can be a great boon for family-controlled businesses which want to stay that way, but would like to raise some outside capital. Majority owners of unquoted companies get full inheritance tax relief, and the Inland Revenue has accepted that companies on AIM and OFEX are unquoted, and thus eligible.

Roll-over Relief

More important, perhaps, is roll-over relief. This makes it possible to defer virtually indefinitely any capital gains tax on qualifying shares bought on the AIM or the OFEX because they are accepted as shares in an unquoted company. So long as the proceeds from the sale of shares in an unquoted company are re-invested in another qualifying unquoted company within three years, no gains tax is payable until after the final sale.

You need to check with your taxman or accountant for full details. Most trading companies qualify, but the Revenue has been predictably difficult in drawing the lines. Some companies which investors had assumed would qualify have been declared ineligible. Those which do not qualify include companies dealing in commodities, futures, banking, insurance or money-lending services, plus a few other related trades. When you finally sell and do not re-invest, you pay gains tax on the total gain at that stage. If your final investment has proved a dud, then your potential bill on the earlier deal will be reduced accordingly. In effect, this means that instead of playing with 60% of your money because you have paid 40% gains tax, you play with 100% of your cash, courtesy of the taxman — more capital on which you might make gains. It does not go all of the way towards counter-balancing the extra risks of investing in an unquoted AIM or OFEX company. But it certainly helps.

It may also be possible to offset losses on shares in qualifying companies against income tax for the year in question, or against income for the previous year. This may not be straightforward. Tax inspectors in some areas apparently dispute it. If it concerns you, take advice.

Small Is Dangerous

There is no point trying to fool yourself. Tax breaks or not, investing in AIM or OFEX companies carries more dangers than most, simply because the companies are smaller. Such companies are first to suffer in a recession, most easily squeezed by bigger competition, less able to cope with changes in the law (these days European Union rules are a real hazard for small companies), and most vulnerable to the mood of their bankers.

Some of the small companies on these markets may also be start-up businesses, or near start-ups. These are yet more dangerous. A high proportion of start-ups go bust within the early years of trading. Even those which make it to the stockmarket in some form are not assured of survival. No amount of apparently impressive professional advice can guarantee success. It is a clear rule for any new project — from Eurotunnel down to a local repair shop — that costs will be higher than expected, and revenue will flow more slowly than planned. Everyone knows it, and yet it rarely seems to be built into even the most sophisticated business plan. Count yourself lucky if the company you choose can escape from that.

Dealing Difficulties

Any AIM or OFEX company may face pretty tough trading problems, but for the investor, there are extra worries. Stock Exchange incompetence and lack of will may have played a part, but the real reason why previous efforts at establishing small company share markets have failed is because of dealing difficulties. They arose purely and simply because when the going got tough, everyone ran for the exit. There was not enough money to be made in a falling market, so the most significant players simply chopped their staff and gave up playing.

There is nothing surprising nor particularly blameworthy about that. Like everyone else, City folk are in business to make money. If they see a fall in activity, and are faced with a flood of sellers of small company shares, they do not want to buy. They are reluctant to sit taking shares on their dealing books, committing money to investments no one wants.

So when the market turns down, it will be more difficult to deal in small company shares. It may be well-nigh impossible at times. That could bring some companies down, stopping them raising extra cash they might need to survive. The whole system feeds upon itself. A lack of confidence in one area spawns a lack of confidence in another, the buying stops, and we all fall down.

As the AIM develops, there are bright hopes, brave resolutions. The pioneers such as J.P. Jenkins and Winterflood Securities are trying hard, and have been joined by others in expanding the market. But if the economy gets too tricky, some market-makers may disappear. Dealing in small company shares may become difficult once again. You could be left with shares you cannot sell in companies which eventually go bust.

Dealing Minuses

This is the biggest minus — the lack of liquidity. Super-looking companies whose shares have performed brilliantly may be clinging to a totally insubstantial dealing base. You may find that the share price is quoted by a couple of market-makers in what appears a reasonable size. The price could be, say, 95p to 100p in 1,000 or 2,500 shares.

That would not be particularly good by normal market standards. A 5% spread is not unusual, but in leading shares, it could be 2% or less. So you start with one disadvantage — the dealing spread is wide. It means that the share has to rise 5% before you are breaking even on price, never mind commission charges. And if the first move after you buy is down, you might suddenly find you are looking at a 10% loss — a price which was 95p to 100p might be 90p to 95p. If you sold, you would only get 90p for shares which cost 100p.

Then you might find that if you bought 2,500 shares on a good day, the market-maker has taken fright for some reason and has cut his dealing size to 1,000 shares. If he is calling the price 90p to 95p in 1,000 shares, he may call it 88p to 97p in 2,000, or even 87p to 98p in 2,500. If you want to sell your 2,500, you might get only 87p.

If the main market has taken a turn for the worse, he might be very reluctant to buy 2,500 at all. He might call a token price of 80p to 100p. That really hurts. In extreme circumstances, he might not wish to buy at all. A good broker will be able to help you out. He might be able to sell 1,000 to each of the two market-makers, and shift 2,000 for you. That is if he can act quickly enough, and the second market-maker does not spot that the first was stuffed with stock, and so cut his quotation before your broker can deal.

And The Pluses

Never say you were not warned. The downside can be nasty. Equally, though, the upside can be marvellous. Market-makers are not evil chaps, out to beat you down at every turn. They are just trying to make a living. Sometimes they will win on a deal, now and then they will lose. So when share prices are rising, they are happy to help. Indeed, they are obliged to.

When it looks good, you will find that market-makers might reduce the spread between buying and selling prices, and might increase the size of lots they will trade. They will also shift prices up quickly in a narrow market stock.

That can be wonderful. If you hold shares in a company where there are buyers but few sellers, market-makers will raise prices rapidly. They want to do business. They have to attract sellers, offer them a good price, so that they can get hold of shares to sell. They cannot afford to risk selling shares they do not have in the hope of buying them more cheaply when a seller appears. A certain amount of that does happen. But it can be expensive for the market-maker if no seller comes forward, and the market-maker has to raise his price and pay more to get stock in.

So just as AIM or OFEX issues can fall sharply in difficult times, they can go up like a rocket in good times. You might find your 95p to 100p price in 1,000 shares becomes 100p to 105p in 1,000, and then 105p to 110p in 2,500. Or even 120p to 125p in 2,500 very quickly.

Watch The Size

It is crucial to keep an eye on market size and the price spread. Unless you are very confident, and ready to hold for the long term, never deal outside the normal size. If the market is normally in 1,000 shares, or perhaps only 500, stick to it as a dealing unit. Otherwise you may have real problems when it comes to selling. If you have 2,500 shares to sell in a 1,000 share market, you may have to take quite a cut in price to shift them.

Happily, more market-makers are venturing into AIM. Almost all stocks have two market-makers, and some have more. It may be possible to deal in, say, 1,000 shares with each of three market-makers. So the market size, if you are brave, could be presented as 3,000 shares, instead of 1,000. Be careful, however. While extra market-makers were picking up the bigger AIM shares in 1995 and 1996, they could walk away if the mood changes.

Penny Shares

You might find sometimes you are trading in penny shares. The strict definition is not important. Some apply it to anything under 100p, others say anything under 20p, or under 10p. It matters not, though in the mid-nineties, it probably refers to shares under 20p.

The point of making a distinction is that such shares have particular attractions, and carry special problems. I have devoted a whole book to the subject, *How To Make A Killing In Penny Shares*, and it has proved enormously popular. Some investors buy only penny shares. Get them right, and they can be marvellous winners.

The Killer Spread

The biggest problem is the dealing spread. This applies with particular force in AIM and OFEX stocks. If you have a share selling at 1p, the price you see in most newspapers and on dealing screens will be the middle price. It might mean that the shares are $^3/_4$p if you want to sell, and $1^1/_4$p to buy. That is a massive $^1/_2$p spread — or 50% of the price.

It might be worse. It is not impossible that a middle price of 1p could conceal a spread between $^1/_2$p to sell, $1^1/_2$p to buy — a real killer.

A good broker should always be able to deal well inside such a spread. A bad one — the kind of pushy salesman or woman who calls you and tries to sell you shares — will exploit it against you ruthlessly.

However you get there, finding a share with such a spread means the odds are loaded against you. It may not sound much, $^1/_4$p or $^1/_2$p, but it is a massive proportion of a penny price. It means the share must move sharply before you are anywhere near breaking even.

It goes higher up the scale, beyond what is literally a penny stock. Take a share at a middle price of 10p. The real price might well be $9^1/_2$p to $10^1/_2$p, a 10% spread. If the first move is down, the share you paid $10^1/_2$p for might get you only 9p back if you sold. Minus commission costs.

So watch out. The spread in penny shares can be a real problem. Never imagine $^1/_2$p is nothing much. If you are buying 100,000 shares — sounds great — that $^1/_2$p move gives you a gain or loss of £500.

Penny shares can be marvellous. Because they feel so good, and you get so many for your money, small investors like them. When they go the right way, they can yield big profits. A rise from 1p to 2p is a gain of 100%, equivalent to something else rising from 150p to 300p, or from 450p to 900p. A rise from 1p to 2p is much more likely than one from 450p to 900p. It can take place on some surge in sentiment alone.

Penny shares do run from 2p to 6p. And back down again. Enjoy them, but be wary. On the AIM and OFEX lists, they are likely to be even more volatile than on the full market. Given the nature of these markets, they are more likely to be newer, more aggressive operations. They could prosper, or collapse more readily. Have fun.

The Winning Ways

It would be wrong to conclude this opening chapter without striking a more positive note. It is essential to emphasise the risks in AIM and OFEX stocks, but it would be wrong to cast too much gloom over everything.

The small company market is built on hope, on expectation, on determination to move forward. There are few burnt-out old businesses struggling to survive, or simply jogging along, going nowhere very special. Merely by choosing to come to the AIM or the OFEX, companies are casting a vote for their future. They are looking towards bigger and better things. If they get it right,

"There are many ambitious businesses growing excited over the opportunity of raising risk capital on reasonable terms"

they could make a lot of money for the proprietors, their employees, and the investors who back them.

In the consultative document on establishing the AIM, the London Stock Exchange vowed it was determined to help stimulate economic growth by ensuring that its markets were accessible to a wide range of companies. It saw AIM as a commitment to supporting and responding to the needs of smaller and growing companies that wished to raise money through shares which could be traded in public.

Behind all of the official posturing, this does illustrate what the AIM is about — helping small companies to grow bigger. That is exciting, and it is a real return to what a stockmarket really ought to be — a place for enterprising businessmen to attract capital from investors ready to take a risk in backing them to build a business. It is where the stockmarket started, hundreds of years ago. And it is an area where the Stock Exchange often appears to have lost its way. The link between private investors and individuals building a business has almost vanished on the main market, where dealings are dominated by remote insurance companies and pension funds, and company bosses are wrapped rigid in red tape.

Make no mistake. The crooks and conmen are jostling for a piece of the AIM and the OFEX action. But there are many ambitious businesses growing excited over the opportunity of raising risk capital on reasonable terms, away from the greedy venture capitalists and the bureaucratic banks.

It can work. It does work. And it can work for you. The Alternative Investment Market might just be the place where the adventurous investor meets the enterprising industrialist — and both come out feeling they have done well on the opportunity market.

2

Are You Ready To Gamble?

Hitting a winning investment puts a new spring into your step. Take no notice of those who pretend to look down on anyone who gambles on shares in the hope of making money, who somehow manage to convey the impression that it is a slightly grubby business. Ignore them. Making money on the stockmarket is marvellous.

And it is so much more than merely making money. The extra cash is wonderful. If you get it right enough, often enough, it can transform your life. People do turn a few hundred pounds into a few thousand. Many succeed in turning a few thousand into tens, even hundreds of thousands. It never ceases to surprise me, the letters from people who say they know little about shares, and who have still somehow got 30/40/50 thousand tied up in them. Or people who come up to me at conferences, and ask what to do about their savings — sometimes a couple of hundred thousand pounds. Somehow they have managed to put a small fortune together, without learning too much about the share market. Simply using their common sense, and perhaps taking a little gamble here and there.

Some have managed to buy property abroad, others have exotic holidays, fancy cars, horses, or are enjoying giving money to their children or grandchildren. The money they have made is providing them with real satisfaction, real enjoyment.

Yet playing the share market is so much more than a way of trying to make money. It is a wonderfully entertaining game. Ignore the po-faced nonsense which attends so much on the City pages, the pretence that is a very serious subject, not to be approached with undue levity. The sheer fun of playing and winning is infectious. Share dealing is a marvellous, highly complex game, whose rules you will never master completely. The money you make when you win is terrific. Never overlook the sheer satisfaction you get from knowing that you were right, bought when so many in the City were selling, or were not paying attention, and that you sold when they were moving in to buy. You lose money — you have lost. Make money, and you have won in a fascinating game.

Never, though, let me suggest that share dealing should be viewed as merely a game. It can be a killer. If you are not properly prepared to play, if you get sucked in and begin to use money you cannot afford to lose, it can become very nasty indeed.

Among the happy letters which lighten my days there are some absolute tales of horror. People do get overstretched. They do borrow to buy shares, and they do sometimes see those shares slump in value. And the worry is quite dreadful. Never do it. NEVER USE MONEY YOU CANNOT AFFORD TO LOSE. NEVER BORROW TO BUY SHARES.

Please heed this warning. This book is littered with warnings about the dangers of the share game. And in looking at the AIM, you are looking at one of the high-risk areas. You can make splendid returns in the AIM. But you can also lose your cash, perhaps almost overnight, with little warning.

Anyone who has read another of my books, *How To Make A Killing In The Share Jungle,* may recall the story there of a colleague. I saw it happen. A smart chap, hired from one of the best financial papers, had a house and a happy marriage when first he joined my office. It was way back in the sixties, at the time of the great Australian mining share boom. I do not know how he did it, but he had to sell his house, and move into a flat. Later, he left financial journalism for a job which would apparently pay more. Next, his marriage hit trouble. Then I lost track of him altogether. He had been playing the share market. Stupidly. It ruined his career, and his marriage.

There were similarly depressing cases all around the City after the Great Share Slump of October 1987, when prices crashed 500 points in two days, and many shares lost a quarter of their value. That disaster struck suddenly. Countless City chaps had to sell their homes, and pull their children out of private education. One trainee accountant lost £1m playing the option market — though the fault lay as much with the bank which allowed him to play as with any foolishness he brought to the table.

So please be aware of what you are doing when you read this book, and when you might fancy your luck on the AIM. You are taking a risk with your money. You could lose the lot.

Just as sure as any punter who puts a fiver on the nose of the Derby favourite, you are gambling. Others may call it investment, simply because the chips you are using are shares. Rubbish. Playing the stockmarket is gambling, no matter what language anyone uses to try to disguise it. You may not lose your stake the instant another winner passes the post, but you could lose it. Prepare yourself accordingly.

Do not kid yourself. Buying any share is risky. Companies do go bust. When they do, shareholders almost always lose all of their investment. Buying any share on the AIM or the OFEX really is riskier than most.

The Financial Fundamentals

Before you begin, be sure you have the financial fundamentals securely in place. Make sure that, if you lose the lot playing the share game, it will not do you serious damage. No matter how careful you are, how lucky you feel, you will lose money on some deals. There is no way around it. And if your string of losses comes at the beginning of your investment adventure, you could wipe out all the cash you have set aside to play.

Whatever you do, make sure your home is safe. You should always have enough to cover the mortgage or the rent each month. Take out proper insurance. A mortgage guarantee policy is essential, covering the cost of repaying your mortgage if you should die, ensuring that the house is left free of debt for your spouse and family. Take out a policy which will ensure that mortgage payments are maintained should you fall ill or suffer some disability. Consider whether you need one which will keep up your mortgage payments if you lose your job.

It is easy to say, but in practice finding a policy which covers all of these things sensibly is quite difficult. The financial services industry has not served us well. Too many policies have dreadful loopholes, allowing insurers to shrug off responsibility just when you need them most.

Do not try to be too adventurous. Go to a big, well-established company, one which has been going for at least 25 years. Ask for advice through a proper independent financial adviser, or your bank or building society. Or stick to some big name such as the Prudential, General Accident, Legal & General, Eagle Star, Norwich Union, Standard Life, or Sun Alliance.

This list is not intended to be comprehensive. It omits several fine, solid companies. But it gives you an idea of where to look. No guarantees. Some of these companies will sometimes serve you badly. Every company has its lapses. But by opting for solid, long-established giants, you are more likely to get a reasonable deal. It may not be the very best — but at least they are likely to be there still if you should ever need them. And they are unlikely to lead you astray deliberately.

You should also go to them for general life insurance, covering three or four times your annual salary if you can afford it. Be sure to join a pension scheme — preferably one offered by your employer. Most schemes offered by big companies are sound. If you are likely to change jobs frequently, opt for a portable pension which will stay with you as you move.

Savings

You should also have some cash set aside for that rainy day. You will need it, eventually. Once again, do not try to be too clever. Safety first is the unshakeable rule. Pop some cash into a building society account, or the National Savings Investment Bank.

Do not worry too much about earning an extra half point or so of interest. It is no good taking a risk for a few pence more, or tying up your money so that you cannot get it out when you need it without sacrificing a chunk of the interest you have earned. Safety and convenience matter most. So go to the local branch of something big. Sadly, the banks often struggle to keep up, and many of their accounts yield miserable returns.

Personal Equity Plans

Once the basic support system is in place, it makes sense to tiptoe towards the share market. Other forms of investment may offer an apparent high return — in the mid-nineties there has been a proliferation of income bonds, many of a somewhat dubious nature — but they do little to preserve your capital against inflation.

You might believe that inflation will not be a major problem in future, with the Governor of the Bank of England apparently determined above all else to beat it out of the system. You would be wrong to trust him. If inflation is laid low forever, wonderful. More likely, though, it will creep back sooner or later. So you need some savings which offer the prospect of capital growth. Equities

— shares in public companies — are the conventional answer. And the Personal Equity Plan is a convenient means of getting into equities with the benefit of exemption from taxes.

The figures change from time to time, but you are allowed to put up to £6,000 a year into a general PEP, and an additional £3,000 into a PEP investing in the shares of a single company. Provided you keep the cash in for a year, capital gains and dividend income are free of tax.

The snag is that all PEPs must have a manager. This means that some City chap takes fees from you for looking after the PEP. In many cases, that wipes out any tax saving. Some managers make the investment choices for you, while in others, you can choose the shares yourself. There are tedious restrictions on which shares can go in — not overseas shares, nor warrants, nor even Government securities. And certainly not AIM or OFEX shares. The 1994 Budget, though, let corporate bonds, Preference shares and convertibles in.

A PEP is valuable, however, to those who want to create a tax-free nest-egg for retirement. It can be used to create a pool of capital from which interest or gains can be taken without incurring tax. And regular investors, who put in £6,000 each year, can eventually amass a worthwhile sum which will yield far greater tax savings than the costs.

Several PEP investors, putting cash in each year to exploit the allowance for a husband and wife, have already squirrelled away more than £100,000 in a tax-free home.

Unit Trusts

At this stage, however, anyone putting the financial fundamentals in place should find it best not to open a PEP as a way into shares, but as a tax-efficient way into either a unit trust or an investment trust. Both can be used as a relatively low-risk way of enjoying the benefits of proper investment management and a trouble-free route round the paperwork in share dealing.

Unit trusts employ managers to buy shares with the cash from individual investors who buy the units. Those managers pick the shares to buy for the trust, and the price of the units moves up or down in line with the value of the shares in the trust. There is a management fee — usually between 1% and $1^1/_2$ % a year, plus a margin for the trust company. This is covered in a spread between the buying price and the selling price of the units, and usually yields efficient trusts about 6%. In certain circumstances, it can be much higher — so watch out.

The size of the trust expands and contracts as investors put money in or take it out by buying or selling units. Most trusts will hold between 40 and 120 different shares, so when you buy a unit, you effectively become the owner of a tiny stake in 40 to 120 companies. The more units you buy, the bigger your stake.

The idea is that by spreading your money over a range of shares, the risk of suffering one or two duds will be reduced, so the units are relatively safe. The disadvantage is, of course, that if the manager spots a massive winner, the impact of the gain will be diminished by the more pedestrian performance of the other shares.

Unit trusts are strictly regulated, and though there have been a few nasty moments, they can be considered relatively secure. Managers do not run off with your money, and they usually follow sensible policies. That is not to say you might not lose quite a lot of money in them. Buy into a trust where the manager is having a poor run, or into one which specialises in a sector of the market which is doing badly, and you could see the value of your stake fall sharply.

When you are attempting to put the fundamentals in place to allow yourself the luxury of gambling on the AIM, you do not want extra risk in your unit trust. So pick a general trust, a safety-first one, from a long-established manager. Go for the middle of the road. Among managers, consider people like M & G, Save & Prosper, Fidelity, Legal & General, or Mercury. Or perhaps Perpetual, the most impressive management group over the past decade. As with anything in investment, there can be no guarantees. Even the best groups are liable to have a few duds.

On the whole, you should steer away from management groups which do not have a long-established tradition. And away from the smaller groups, which may flatter for a while, but may not achieve sustainable performance.

Equally, I have an aversion to specialist trusts, those designed to invest in shares from just one area of industry — gold mining, for example — or just one geographical area. China is the latest fashion. They have their place, but only in the portfolio of sophisticated investors who already have a wide range of other investments. Even then, they should account only for a small proportion of that portfolio. Watch out. It cannot be long before we see funds offering a way into the Russian market, where gun-law and corruption is the dominant factor.

One other warning. Do not buy any trust which is not based in this country. Perfectly respectable management groups have subsidiaries operating from Jersey or the Isle of Man for what appear to be perfectly good reasons, usually involving tax saving. The vast number of them are sound. But how do you spot the duds? Avoid the Isle of Man, especially. Stick to the mainland.

Open-ended Investment Companies

We are soon to get a new variety of unit trust, the open-ended investment company. These will have substantially the same qualities as those outlined above for unit trusts, but will have a single price for both buying and selling. Treat them as you would a unit trust in assessing their merits.

Investment Trusts

Many of the comments which apply to unit trusts apply also to investment trusts. The two are similar, and often share management groups and fund managers. The difference is in their structure, and that influences the way their prices move.

Whereas the size of a unit trust is determined by the amount of money which flows in and out from investors, investment trusts have a fixed, clearly defined capital structure. They raise money by selling shares in themselves, and use that pool of money to buy shares which the managers think will do well.

From time to time, they may raise extra capital by issuing new shares — usually called "C" shares — but these issues are infrequent. If they take place, it may be only once in a decade.

Because the number of shares in the investment trust is limited, their price responds to supply and demand. The better the managers fare with their investments, the higher the underlying value of the trust. In theory, that attracts greater demand for the shares in the trust itself, so their price rises. Obviously, poor performance is likely to start sellers, and lead to a lower share price for the trust.

In practice, the price of investment trust shares has often been well below the value of the investments they hold. That is known as the discount-to-asset value. Twenty years ago, that discount was over 30% on some large and well-managed trusts. In recent years, more acute management, better marketing, and clever incentive schemes have cut discounts sharply, and there have been brief periods when some shares have sold above the value of their underlying investments — a premium. That usually tends to be a matter of fashion.

Clearly, when investment trust shares sell at a premium, it is best to plump for the equivalent unit trust. No sense in paying more than the shares are worth when the corresponding unit trust sells for exactly what the units are worth. In times when investment trust discounts are more than 5% or so, they are the

"Beware of new management groups, unduly specialised trusts — and those based overseas"

better value than unit trusts. You can get 100p worth of assets, or more, for 95p.

Most of the warnings which apply to unit trusts apply also to investment trusts — beware of new management groups, unduly specialised trusts, those based overseas. And, safety first, stay clear of so-called split-level trusts. These divide their capital into various classes — capital shares, income shares, zero coupon bonds, and so on. These have their virtues, but you need to know exactly what you are doing when you play in such areas.

What you want is a simple Ordinary share in a large, well-established general growth investment trust — something like Foreign & Colonial Investment Trust (not one of the many other Foreign & Colonial trusts) or Alliance, or Witan, or the like.

Popping Into PEPs

Be clear, though. You do not want to buy investment trusts or unit trusts in straightforward fashion. You can, of course, but it is better to pop them into a PEP and enjoy the benefits they offer without being subject to tax. Most management groups have facilities to help you set up a PEP to hold their shares.

Monthly Plans

If you fancy more exposure to the general share market in relatively safe fashion, all well and good. Most investment and unit trusts offer monthly savings plans. These can be very useful for the inexperienced investor, or someone who wants hassle-free exposure to the stockmarket in relatively low-risk fashion.

The plans commit you to a regular monthly subscription which is put into the investment trust shares or the unit trust in small, regular sums. It exploits the virtues of what is known as pound cost-averaging. This classic jargon covers a simple notion. It means you do not have to worry whether the market is up or down when you buy. Because you are committed to a fixed amount each month, you buy fewer shares or units when prices are up, more when they are down.

In theory, this is excellent. You always want to buy more when prices are low. This does it for you. It also averages out your buying cost. So at the end of the year, you have neither put in all your cash at the top, nor at the bottom. You look somewhere sensible, on the average.

Where it does count, of course, is when you decide to sell. If you are taking a long-term view — and in this instance you should — the chances are that you will be able to sell when the market is doing relatively well, and you will have a profit. Over the medium to long term — say five years or so — the market usually shows a gain. Over 10 years or more, there is almost a guarantee, especially if you have been pound cost-averaging. Of course, unless you need the money for something special at some specific time, you can always hold on until the market does pick up. No matter how gloomy things may seem at the time, the depression never lasts. In the end, no matter what they say, market slump is always followed by a market boom. The trick is to sell in the boom before the slump rolls around again.

Getting It Right

Putting your insurance, mortgages, savings, PEPs, units trusts and investment trusts in place may sound boring, a tedious business. You did not buy a book about making money in the AIM to be lectured about such stuff. Too bad. It would be wildly irresponsible not to deliver such a lecture, and of you to disregard it.

It would be impossible for me to write a book like this without it. My conscience would not allow it. Whatever happens, you must put your safety systems in place before you embark on the high-risk, high-reward investment adventure which this book opens up. Please believe me. Bitter experience tells me to hammer on about it. In over 30 years as a financial journalist, I have read the letters, met the poor people who have disregarded these lessons through ignorance or impetuosity.

Usually, it is too late for me — or anyone else — to help. They have lost money they could not afford to lose, and landed themselves in a sorry state. A moment or two of optimism or plain greed has cost them dear.

Do not let this happen to you. Get the fundamentals right. They will stand you in good stead. If you are lucky, you will never need to think about them again. But if ever you get in trouble with your job or your mortgage, need to claim against a life insurance policy, or simply have to find the cash for some emergency, you will be grateful that you set your affairs in order from the beginning.

Can You Cope?

There is more. Less easily defined, but probably almost as important. You have to decide whether you can really cope with playing the AIM. It is, once again, a high-risk, high-reward game. You might not be ready for that — or perhaps your partner might not be. This is no joke. The financial trauma is one thing. The emotional cost quite another.

Think about it. Never try to fool yourself. Buying any share is a gamble, no matter what they try to tell you. Buying any share on the AIM is very much a gamble. You will be gambling. You will become a gambler.

Gambling can become an obsession. It is easy to get sucked in, enticed by the notion that you will be lucky, that you can get it right, that surely it must be your turn to make a killing if you keep trying long enough. And when you make a gain or two, you may become convinced that you have cracked it. One win and you may think you can score again if you just keep trying, find a little more cash.

So be careful. Playing the stockmarket can become a drug. It can take over your life, ruin your marriage. You will certainly become elated if you do hit a winner, and deflated, perhaps depressed, when you back a loser.

Set yourself a limit in advance, decide how much you are prepared to lose. Maybe you will lose the lot, or most of it, fairly quickly. Beginner's luck does not always work. If that happens, walk away. Give it up. Playing this game is not for you.

Tell Your Partner

If you are married, please let your spouse have some idea of what you are doing. No need to report every up and down, even every investment. That could involve your partner in unnecessary worry. But do tell him or her that you plan to gamble in shares, and give him/her an idea of how much you plan to commit to the game. It might just transform your lives. A sensible partner will be a help, sharing your triumphs, perhaps exerting an essential restraining influence if you are tempted to risk too much.

How Much Do You Need?

There is no need to commit a fortune if you want to play. Sometimes people say they plan to put £100 into a couple of shares. Good luck. Ideally, that is too little, because the costs of buying and selling will eat up perhaps £20 or more of that before you start. To make any money, you then need a really spectacular gain.

Never mind. If that is the way you want to play, and you can find a broker who will deal for you on that basis (one of the widely advertised share shops might be most likely) good luck. Once or twice, I have put £150 each into a share for my children as a long-odds speculation. If you are prepared to recognise that it is an expensive way of playing, so be it.

It is more sensible, though, to deal in larger lots. Around £1,000 a time seems good to me, though £500 might do. The charges for investing £1,000 are scarcely more than investing £100. As a proportion of the overall cost, they are much less, of course. And you do not need to worry about putting just one lot of £1,000 into just one share, and nothing else. Do it, if you want. Obviously the more you can put up, the more companies you can invest in, the greater the chance of picking a winner. Or a loser. Whatever takes your fancy, so long as you do it with your eyes open.

Spreading The Risk

It is simple common sense to try to spread the risk. It does dilute the impact of a big winner, of course. It is hard enough to pick one super share, let alone two or three. But you should try. Obviously the more you pick, the better your chances of hitting the big one. Crucially, though, you are sure to make mistakes, especially when you start. There will be shocks along the way. Some of your real bankers may go wrong. So try to spread your money over three or four different stocks, at least.

Insider Trading

When you decide whether you are equipped to go ahead consider, too, how you feel about playing the game with one hand tied behind your back. And maybe a ball and chain attached to your ankle.

The simple truth is that you will not be competing on a fair and equal basis. The most obvious disadvantage is that you will be dealing in a market where the most effective players have inside knowledge.

Tut, tut. Illegal, that, surely? Everyone is supposed to have equal access to all information at the same time. Anyone who trades on the basis on privileged, price-sensitive information should go directly to jail. And every so often there are stories of how the Stock Exchange has come up with some wonderful computing power to help ferret out wrong-doers.

Fuzzy logic, the latest computer system is called. It supports some pretty fuzzy logic in official thinking, too.

The truth is that, no matter how much they try, the authorities will never stop insider dealing. They may make it more difficult. They have closed some of the more obvious loop-holes, and achieved enough to deter some of the villains. Everyone is certainly a lot more careful now.

Sadly, though the Exchange has a good idea of who is up to what, it has proved impossible to prosecute effectively. The boys are still at it, and likely always to continue. It is uncanny how frequently prices edge up or down in advance of significant news. Someone knows, someone deals.

As a private investor, you are unlikely ever to benefit from insider information. You may get gossip. Some of it may be right, some wrong. If you ever get the real thing, stumble across genuine privileged, money-making information, forget it. Do not touch the shares concerned. You will get caught. Small punters are the easiest to trap. While others may cheat, you should never be tempted. Insider dealing is unfair, immoral, immensely frustrating — and pointless to worry about. If you cannot accept that it is part of the game, forget the stockmarket.

Everyone Has An Angle

Always remember that you will be competing with insiders. Use it to remind yourself of another of my favourite stockmarket rules — everyone has an angle.

That sounds like the weary reaction of a tired old sceptic. Maybe. Treat it as the fruits of experience, and turn it to your advantage. Someone, somewhere, always knows more than you do. They understand the system better, and will beat you every time if you cross them.

Go with it, though, and you can benefit. As a journalist, my angle is pretty feeble. I would quite like you to say something nice to my boss, to secure my job. It was brilliant when a flood of letters and calls from readers persuaded the *Daily Mail* to restore my share-tipping column after changes on the paper knocked it out for a while in the spring of 1996. And it suits me if you carry on buying the newspaper I write for. As an author, I would be pleased if you buy this book. Those are my angles. Pretty small beer.

Your stockbroker wants to earn commission from you. It suits him for you to buy or sell, rather than to sit tight. In certain circumstances, it might suit him and his firm for you to buy a particular share. Company directors want you to believe in them so that you will buy their products, and their company's shares.

They employ public relations companies to spread favourable information, or suppress other items. And so on.

Nothing sinister, most of the time. It is the way of the world. Keep it in mind. If you are going to gamble in the share market, it pays to become just a little less trusting, a shade more sceptical. Everyone has an angle. If you can spot it, perhaps you can exploit it, perhaps you can see a way it will help you to make money, score points in the game. Or perhaps you may realise that you should simply stay away from certain situations.

Always ask yourself what is in it for the other party, and whether it means there could be something in it for you. And see if it could help you to win the great share game — a game with a vocabulary all its own.

3

Learning
The Language

Becoming a shareholder is easy. All you need is a little cash, the name of someone who will buy for you, and a share to buy. Most of the twelve million shareholders in the UK have found it even simpler still. They have stuck to privatisation issues in the great state sell-off. They have simply filled in the form in the paper, posted it off with a cheque, and sat back as the dividends and capital gains have rolled in.

It has been marvellous. Easier than reading a Jeffrey Archer novel. In its eagerness to get the nation to buy, the Government has resolutely under-priced almost every issue. The profits have simply poured in, and people who would normally never go near the stockmarket have developed into affluent absentee capitalists — absent by virtue of their lack of understanding and concern for what has actually been going on. Only in the mid-nineties have some come to appreciate that as shareholders they might have a small say in halting the greedy rewards privatised water and electricity bosses have been securing for themselves. And a few have woken up to find the regulators developing teeth, causing nasty problems for British Gas, and the odd wrong number for British Telecom.

If you are among the privatisation profit-makers, congratulations. But do not be deceived. It is not that easy elsewhere in the share jungle. The risks are vastly greater, and you need to know much more to have a chance of succeeding. Unless you are plain lucky.

The lucky investor beats all. From time to time, various magazines or newspapers have set the professionals to compete against the random investor. The pros have picked stocks, and the opposition has thrown darts at a price list, spun a wheel, or something else. Sometimes the professionals come out ahead. Sometimes. Quite often, the lucky throw wins.

If you want to rely on luck alone, fair enough. It is your decision. But be aware of what you are doing. Eventually, luck runs out. Knowledge and judgement can offer no guarantees. But they do tip the odds in your favour.

The more you understand, the better your chances. After more than 30 years as an investor and a journalist with privileged access to all sorts of experts and information, I still make sorry mistakes from time to time. Anyone who tells you I recommended Polly Peck near the top, months before the collapse, is right. My mistake was shared by commentators on most newspapers, and analysts galore in stockbroking offices. Although I continue to believe that Polly Peck and Asil Nadir were shamefully treated by the authorities, I made a bad mistake in forgetting my normal rule. I failed to tell investors to cut their losses as Polly shares began to slide. Perhaps I have learnt from it. I hope so.

In fact, my average is pretty good. But even now, it is clear that there is always too much to learn. It is hard to catch up with all the lessons from the past, harder still to keep abreast of new ideas. But it does pay to try.

Do not be put off by the apparent complexity of the investment world. The City retains an intimidating air, mixing money, power, tradition and mystery which can overwhelm the outsider. Once inside, it can be broken down to the familiar mixture of fear and greed, ambition and industry, and sometimes incompetence and improvisation.

There are many dedicated, intelligent, understanding individuals in the City. Some of our brightest brains are there, equipped with all the aids that money can buy. But they breathe and bleed like the rest of us. They make mistakes, sometimes of a surprisingly elementary nature. And most City folk are just like the rest of us, insecure and uncertain at times, trying to make the best of things. They get a little muddled now and then, and do not always quite understand what they are doing.

Using Your Head

All that really matters to you is that you should understand what you are doing and why you are doing it. Use your common sense. If it does not seem right to you, perhaps it is not right. If it does not make sense, do not assume that some clever chap in the City has worked it out, so it must be right. Perhaps he got it wrong. Or

"Use your common sense. If it does not seem right to you, perhaps it is not right"

perhaps — and this really can come hammering home in the speculative end of the stockmarket — it has been designed that way. Perhaps you have spotted the flaw simply by using your head. Believe me, it happens. Would common sense have told you not to invest in a project farming angora goats in Scotland? A well-known name promoted just such a scheme. Several highly paid City chaps invested in it. It took one, maybe two years to fall apart. And investing in ostriches? Would you believe it? Thousands did. Use your common sense.

Make Sure You Understand

Above all, be sure it makes sense to you. Ask questions. If you cannot understand the answers, walk away. If it all seems improbable to you, leave it alone. If you cannot quite put your finger on what is wrong, but it makes you uneasy, forget it. Someone wants you to buy, to part you from your money. They have an angle. If they cannot make the advantages clear enough to you, too bad. Never hesitate to ask, and ask again until you do understand. There are all sorts of sophisticated sales courses, deliberately designed to wriggle around the objections of people just like you. Some use techniques designed to make you feel silly even asking questions, let alone persisting with them. Never mind. Above all, be sure you get the answers you need. Never let anyone blind you with science, or gently imply you may be half a slice short when using your loaf. Leave it.

If you do get it wrong, buy something you were not completely happy about, you will be the one who loses money. You will be the fool for failing to persist with the questions. Never worry if it becomes apparent that you are venturing into an area which you genuinely will not be able to grasp, no matter how often it is explained. It happens to all of us. Shrug it off. If it gets too tricky for you to follow, leave it to those who can comprehend. Walk away.

Translating The Share-speak

Anyone contemplating the share game will recognise, however, that you need to be able to understand the basics before you can begin asking reasonable questions. You ought to learn the language. As you go along, it will become less daunting. So will the sums. The figure-work never need be a problem. You rarely have to do much of it yourself. There is usually someone else who has done it first. The basics are available in many newspapers and magazines. And your broker will have electronic information services at his fingertips, ready to help, if you ask nicely.

So do not worry if you do not know how to work out a price-earnings ratio, or a dividend yield. They are easily available, a couple of the routine standards by which shares are judged. It is how you use them, not whether you can work them out yourself, which matters.

What Is A Share?

Starting from the very beginning, you need to know just what is a share. Simple, really. A share is a piece of paper which entitles you to a part of a business. If four people agree to form a company, and each puts £25 towards a £100 company, and each takes a corresponding slice, there will be four shares of equal value. If a fifth person joins, and they agree that he will run the business for them on an equal basis, they might give him a share. So there will be five shares, each of the same value, though four have put in cash, and one is offering his skills.

You can slice the shares up any way you fancy. There might be five shares worth a nominal £20 each, or perhaps there might be 100 shares each valued at £1. Each of our five company promoters might take 20 shares apiece. Obviously public companies are vastly larger and more complicated than this, and have arrived at their present share structures by a more complex route. But the basic rule remains — a share represents a piece of a company. The more shares you have, the bigger piece you have. Though there are some strict variations in definition, most people use "stocks" and "shares" as if they were identical terms.

Nominal Value

In the UK, all shares must have a nominal — or par — value. It does not really matter what it is. Some giants have shares with a 25p nominal value, others are £1, and some 1p.

That bears no direct relevance to the market value of the shares. A 1p nominal value share selling for 60p is no dearer or cheaper than a 25p nominal value share which also sells for 60p. All that matters in determining value is the market price, what someone will pay for it. Never be put off because someone tells you a particular share is selling for 500p and has only a par value of 25p.

Dividends

The only real area where par, or nominal value, has any relevance is when it comes to reporting dividends. A dividend is the money paid out to shareholders each year. It usually comes from profits, though sometimes companies will pay from reserves accumulated from past profits.

Dividends are usually described as so many pence, or fractions of pence, per share. Or expressed as a percentage of the par value of the shares. So a dividend might be 1p a share. If the share has a nominal value of 1p, then that 1p dividend will be a dividend of 100%. If the par value is £1, that 1p will be a dividend of 1%. If you hold the shares, the percentage does not matter. You still get 1p for each share.

Most shares are called Ordinary shares (as distinct from those with special rights), or equities. Dividends are the equivalent to the interest you earn from a fixed interest account, like a building society account or such, and broadly speaking they rise or fall in line with profits each year. Most companies pay two dividends each year, an interim, or half-year dividend, and a final, or full-year dividend. In many cases, the final is larger than the interim payment. There is often a long delay between the dividend being announced and cheques being sent out.

Sometimes companies offer scrip dividends. These mean you can take extra shares instead of cash dividends. That can have tax advantages, and saves you the dealing costs of buying more. It saves the company from paying out cash when it needs money — though it does create extra shares on which dividends will have to be paid indefinitely.

Fixed Interest Capital

Most companies have some form of fixed interest capital alongside their Ordinary shares. This is a different way of raising money. Most fixed interest securities pay a set rate of interest each year, and have a prior claim on the assets of the company should it be wound up. Interest on fixed interest capital has to be paid whether profits rise or fall. The most common forms are Preference stocks, Convertible Loan stocks, or Loan stocks. In general, they will appeal more to those seeking a secure, higher income than anyone hunting capital gains.

Share Certificates And Contract Notes

It has been normal for investors to receive a share certificate from the registrars of any company specifying how many shares they own. In the middle of 1996, a new system came in to do away with share certificates on issues after that date, though earlier certificates will carry on, and it will be possible to get certificates at extra cost. They will, however, be phased out, being replaced by computer entries. While they last, certificates offer legal proof of ownership, and you must send them to your broker whenever you sell shares. So they need to be kept somewhere safe.

As soon as you buy or sell, your broker sends a contract note, confirming how many shares have been traded, at what price, and listing other charges. Keep it. Unless you are dealing within a PEP, you may need to confirm the details for tax purposes.

The Investment Calendar

Companies normally follow a predictable annual routine, doing the same things at roughly the same time each year. There will be a half-year, or interim, profit statement, accompanied by news of the interim dividend. Increasingly companies include a balance sheet, giving an idea of their borrowing levels and asset strength.

Between two and three months after the end of the company's trading year — which need not be the same as the calendar year — the company will usually announce how profits have fared in the full year. That statement will carry news of the final dividend. Often called the preliminary profits announcement, strictly speaking, it is not fully audited by the accountants who watch over things on behalf of shareholders. In practice, it is hardly ever changed. Nothing will be sent direct to investors at that stage, though the announcement will appear on the electronic news services in all broking offices around the City, other screen news services, and in the press.

A short while later, the company will post the annual report and accounts to shareholders. It can range from a bare 20-page affair to a glossy 80-page epic, fat with colour pictures of the group's operations around the world, and even shiny portraits of the chairman protected by soft tissue inserts.

That can speak volumes about the company, though not perhaps in the way intended. The glossier and more exotic, the greater the care investors need. A degree of promotion is welcome. It shows the company recognises the value of getting the message across to everyone, an angle investors must approve. Too much, though, suggests more shadow than substance. And too much boardroom narcissism might suggest the directors are losing their sense of values, growing to believe their own publicity.

What Is In The Accounts

The report and accounts is worth careful attention, both for the message it conveys by its style, and for the hard facts it carries. There is a major draw-back, of course. Every line is out of date by the time you get it. The figures cover a year which has gone, and whose impact has already influenced the share price. The balance sheet is a picture of how things were on the day the trading year ended, not how they may have been a day earlier, or a day later. Sometimes the difference can be crucial. The importance of arranging things to look good on that one day does not escape company managements. Even the most strait-laced folk must be tempted to look their best when they know everyone will be looking at them.

Centre-piece of the report — or so he would like to think — is the chairman's statement. Often this contains little more than the broadest generalisations about how the business is faring. If it gives any clue to the future, it will be of the blandest kind. Read it, though. Anything which may give you a broader grasp of the business is useful.

Nowadays, there is often a report from the chief executive. That goes into more specifics. Some also have divisional directors chipping in.

The Directors' Report

The directors' report is usually a colourless affair, but worth investigating for details of personnel changes at the top, and of how many shares the directors hold. It also gives details of anyone holding more than 3% of the capital of the company — useful if there should be bid rumours. Sometimes the big stakeholder is a bidder. Sometimes it indicates that there may be several potential sellers around if a bidder should emerge. Or perhaps a powerful trading partner is backing the business.

Corporate Governance

These days, there is also some nonsense about corporate governance and the Cadbury Committee. This is meant to assure you that the board conducts its affairs in proper fashion, with committees to control this, that and the other. Take no notice unless it shows that some overpaid brigand from another company or some merchant bank is in charge of deciding board pay. Even then, there is precious little you can do but complain. And that will make little practical difference.

The Auditors' Report

There will be an auditors' report, signed by a firm of accountants, telling you that everything is true and fair and complies with the Companies Act and so on. If there is anything seriously awry, the auditors will have spotted it.

If they should qualify their report in any way, look out. If it says the company is operating on a going concern basis, that probably indicates the business is relying on its banks for loans which might be withdrawn. Such notes are normally self-explanatory now. By the time you see them, the rest of the investment world will know about them, and the shares will be rated accordingly. Not everyone gets the ratings right.

There may be more need to worry than the market thinks. You can bet that if there is any qualification in the accounts, it is serious. The directors will have pulled every trick possible to try to persuade the auditors not to make it public. Do not put a penny into such a company unless you are sure you understand what the qualification is about, and can be sure that it does not mean trouble ahead. If you already hold the shares, sell at once unless you can set your mind at rest. Why take a risk?

Profit And Loss Account

The report will also carry a profit and loss account, most of which will already have been published with the preliminary announcement. There will be pages of notes, expanding on this. Read them, and the statement of accounting policies, carefully. They will give you more insight into what is going on.

Balance Sheet

The accounts come with a balance sheet which shows what the company owns and what it owes at the end of the trading year. That is important, because it indicates how the cash has been flowing in and out of the business, and what would be left for shareholders if the business was wound up. In practice, though, things are very different. Later in the book, we examine how to learn more from the balance sheet, and the notes to the accounts.

The Annual Meeting

The report will also carry notice of the time and place of the annual meeting. As a shareholder, you are entitled to go along and ask questions. There will be notice of resolutions to be proposed at the meeting. Most will be routine, asking shareholders to approve the report and accounts, declare a dividend, re-elect a few directors, give the board authority to appoint and pay the auditors, and to issue a certain number of shares should they choose. Watch out for anything different, and make sure you understand what it involves.

Extraordinary Meetings

Sometimes you will receive notice of an extraordinary meeting. This will be required to approve some sizeable deal, raising extra money, or buying or selling a large business. The accompanying document will explain what is going on. As usual, much of the meat may be in the fine print.

As with the annual meeting, you will be sent a card allowing you to cast your votes (one for each share) on the resolutions. Go along, cast them in person if you can. Usually your votes will count for little, but the chance of seeing and meeting the board will be valuable. There is no substitute for weighing directors up face to face.

Absorb that little lot, and you are on the way towards speaking the language of the share game, understanding the evidence. Is it time to set about buying some shares?

4

How To Buy
Alternative Investments

At any stage of the game, you can throw this book aside, close
your eyes, and leap in. You can play the share game on any market
with as much or as little knowledge as you choose. Having got this
far in the book, with a rough idea of what you are talking about,
perhaps you fancy a preliminary peep at how you might play,
even a gentle dabble. After all, you never know. You might get
lucky.

Sounds good? Forget it. The AIM is a little different. Ring your
broker to talk about the AIM, and you might get a flea in your ear
— politely, of course. And the OFEX? Oh my goodness. Investors
used to be put off buying shares because it was difficult to find a
broker to buy for them. Now brokers are all over the place,
advertising for business. That is good news. But many of the most
prominent advertisers are execution-only brokers — they will do
what you tell them, buy and sell cheaply and efficiently for you.

But you have to tell them which share to buy. They do not give advice. That is more expensive and more difficult to find.

When it comes to trading on the AIM or the OFEX, it is much harder to find a sensible way in. Many brokers know little about it, are unfamiliar with the companies, or how to set about buying them. It should not be that way, but that happens with anything new. It remains to see how well the market develops after being adopted by the Stock Exchange in the summer of 1995. Already, using it has become easier. But it could take quite a while before everyone is happy. And before all brokers agree to deal for any but their most experienced clients.

Most brokers will be quick to tell you that the AIM or the OFEX involves high-risk trading. Many disapprove on principle. They will try to steer you into what they consider more suitable areas. Or simply turn you away. You may develop a pretty poor opinion of the London Stock Exchange and some of its members. In some cases, you may be right.

Whatever the frustrations, dealing through a member of the Stock Exchange is much your best bet. Most dealers in most firms are honourable, sensible people, who will genuinely seek to do what they consider best for you. As in every area, there are a few rogues. And there are certainly brokers who are careless and sometimes incompetent. But there are now all manner of rules and regulations, referees and ombudsmen to ensure tolerably fair treatment. Stick with a stockbroker if you can. On the whole, the alternatives are less attractive.

How The Stock Exchange Works

It makes sense for you to spend a little time becoming familiar with how the Exchange works. It will help you conduct your dealings properly, and avoid misunderstandings.

That great grey tower block slap in the centre of the City of London in Throgmorton Street may still be called the Stock Exchange Tower, but precious little business is done there any more. It now houses Stock Exchange officials and stockbroking offices, but no longer boasts an actual trading floor. The six-sided boxes which used to flash up on TV news every so often have long gone, killed by the Big Bang in October 1986 which put an end to a time-honoured system which many still think was superior to the existing operation.

In the old days, brokers used to go to the trading floor, approach the jobbers who used to hold a supply of shares in different companies, and negotiate deals and prices with them. Now it all happens on screens. You see the dealing rooms on TV from time to time. Some pundit delivers his verdict on the economy while a vast hall buzzes away in the background. There are rows of desks, each carrying three or more screens and a battery of telephones, with shirt-sleeved men or earnest women punching keyboards, or shouting down the phone. It looks like a contemporary version of hell. Sometimes it feels like it.

Market-makers

In the old days, there was a split between the broker (who bought or sold on your behalf), and the jobber (who dealt only with brokers and acted as a sort of share wholesaler). Now the same firm can be both broker and jobber, taking your order, and buying shares from you for its own account. Or selling you shares it actually holds.

There are supposed to be barriers — Chinese walls, they call them — stopping this dual capacity operating against the interests of the outsider. As the joke goes, Chinese walls have chinks in them. There are many big investment houses which dream up ideas for bids and deals, put them to the companies they think might carry them out, advise them on how best to do them, buy and sell shares for them in the deals — and carry on dealing in those shares for the rest of the world, wearing another hat. The sums involved can be billions. It is not unusual for some of the smarter firms to make themselves £10m profit in a matter of minutes on a deal to buy and sell a block of shares.

You may believe those who say that this does not present

enormous conflicts of interest, and does not mean outsiders sometimes find that their interests are secondary to those of some other part of the firm. On the other hand, you may not believe it.

Whatever you think, there is little you can do about it. It is a fact of City life. If you disapprove too strongly, stay away.

As it is, the firms which used to be jobbers are now called market-makers. In that role, they act effectively as wholesalers of shares. The market-makers publish on a screen the number of shares they will buy or sell in a particular company, and the price at which they will do it. There may be 16 or more competing market-makers offering to trade in the shares of the biggest companies. At the bottom end, there are supposed to be at least two for every share. In practice, and especially on AIM stocks, there may be one who really sets the price. On OFEX, there certainly will be just one.

There will be a gap between the price at which each market-maker will buy, and the price at which he will sell. That is his turn, or profit. The size of that gap varies. It will be set by relation to the absolute price (obviously a 1p gap between buying and selling prices on a share quoted at around 10p is proportionately larger than a 5p gap on a share selling at around 100p), by relation to the amount of business in that share (more trade means margins can be cut), and the competition (two market-makers might be happy to trade with a gap of, say, 10% between buying and selling prices, whereas competition between four market-makers might reduce the gap to, say, 7%).

Brokers

Some market-making firms are also stockbroking firms. As an individual, you cannot deal direct with a market-maker. You have to use a broker to do it for you. That broker acts as your agent, scanning the prices advertised by market-makers on the screen, and picking where to deal on your behalf. You might feel more confident if his firm is not also a market-maker, and is not acting as principal as well as your agent.

Brokers are supposed to owe you a duty of best execution. That means they should pick the market-maker offering the best terms, and deal with them. Good brokers can sometimes talk their way into getting a better price for you than appears on the screen.

The Touch

Any broker should tell you "the touch" when you ask a price. This is the difference between the best buying price quoted by any market-maker, and the best selling price. Because the market-makers will not all be quoting exactly the same prices for one particular share, it is possible to narrow the margin between buying and selling prices in this way.

Say one market-maker is quoting 90p if you sell, 94p if you buy. The margin would then be 4p between buying and selling prices. Another market-maker may be quoting 89p if you sell, 93p if you buy. Your broker should take the most favourable prices for you — the 90p if you sell, and the 93p if you buy, to make quotation of 90p to 93p. The "touch" then is 3p, not the 4p margin each market-maker is quoting.

The Limited AIM

Unfortunately, talk about "the touch" and such may be wasted on the AIM. You may have to settle for what you can get. There are unlikely to be more than three firms making a market in any individual share, and often one of them will be the sponsor — a broker advising that company on corporate affairs.

All of the problems of conflict of interest apply when you trade on the AIM or the OFEX. Not because there is so much big money involved, but because this is the small-time stuff. Most of those involved do not have massive resources. This is the market for shares in smaller companies, and it is served in turn by smaller City firms.

Obviously smaller means more risk. But it also means that many of those involved are more deeply committed to making it work. It matters more to them than it would to some all-purpose international investment giant who could afford to put a £10m mistake down to petty cash. On the AIM, £10m would breathe life into several firms. Or knock them out of the game completely if they lost it.

So you may find that brokers who are most familiar with the AIM have more than one iron in the fire. They may be ready to buy or sell for you in good faith, doing the best they can for you. But the same broker may effectively be the market-maker in some AIM companies. The firm may buy the shares you want to sell, and hold them for sale to another party. Or it may sell you shares that it is already holding.

It may be the only real dealer in these shares. While there may be one or two other market-makers in theory, the bulk of the business might in practice be done by just one firm. So that firm effectively sets the price.

That same firm may have sponsored the flotation of the company whose shares you are trading in. So it may have a pretty good idea of who owns them, who might be a buyer, who might be a seller. It will also know a great deal about the company's business. It may also be acting as corporate finance adviser, and someone in the broking firm might be privy to the company's plans or problems. If all of these multiple functions exist for most AIM companies, they exist as a matter of routine for almost all OFEX companies, although in OFEX the actual market-maker will independent.

Conflicting Aims

There may, then, be a massive conflict of interest. The warning may sound familiar. Something very like it appears earlier in this book. But it bears repeating. Let me lay it out, in the most extreme form. You may ask a broker to buy shares for you. That broker may be the only effective channel for buying or selling those shares. That broker can choose how many shares he will buy or sell, and can effectively set the price. That same broker may also know of other big buyers or sellers, and may know exactly how well or badly that company is trading, and what it plans to do next.

Sounds pretty rough? There it is. In theory, of course, no broker would be allowed to combine all of those elements and use them to the disadvantage of his client. In theory. There are all sorts of rules and regulators to ensure that it does not happen. In practice? Never say you were not warned.

The Good Guys

It would be irresponsible not to warn would-be AIM or OFEX investors about such worries, and keep on warning them. But it would be equally irresponsible to suggest that the worst abuses intrude too much. Most who operate in these markets will be doing their best to make them work for everyone. Take the gloomiest view — never a bad thing in the investment world — and you realise that they know they will kill the market and their business if trading is seen to be too unfair.

There are good guys galore. In particular, there are two firms which do not have a conflict of interest. They act as market-makers alone, not as corporate sponsors, nor as broker. They provide the bedrock for the AIM.

Others may emerge, but at the beginning, the dominant force is the firm of J.P. Jenkins. It is headed by John Jenkins, a former Stock Exchange jobber, once the specialist in the shares of football clubs. He is one of the most respected figures in the City, never one of the big players, but always a man to be trusted to play his part properly. He became the biggest trader in shares under the old Stock Exchange rule 535.2, which gave birth to the AIM. Jenkins nurtured the 535 market. Instead of simply matching buyers and sellers, he became a market-maker in the shares of perhaps 100 companies, quoting a regular buying and selling price in set quantities.

Realising the importance of proper information, he also set up a supply of regular share prices to the Reuters agency and others to transmit on their City screen services. And he set up a Newstrack service covering the latest announcements from companies in which he was prepared to trade shares.

While this means Jenkins has become a crucial player in the AIM, he has gone on to use his organisation to set up the OFEX, which his firm runs. The Newstrack service now specifically covers OFEX listed companies, not AIM companies.

While Jenkins has emerged as one crucial market-maker in small company shares, Winterflood Securities is also a major player. Brian Winterflood, another enormously respected veteran of the Stock Exchange jobbing system, developed his business as a specialist market-maker catering for smaller companies. Known as "Mr USM" for his support for the short-lived stepping-stone to the main market, he has become a massive power in the AIM. He and Jenkins are splendid pioneers. If either firm is among the market-makers for any AIM company you fancy trading, the chances of being able to buy and sell relatively freely are much improved.

If your broker tells you he has never heard of the shares you wish to trade, and cannot find them quoted, tell him to try Jenkins or Winterflood. The chances are that one of them will be making the market. If not, they will almost certainly know who is.

Finding A Broker

Your hair may curl at the thought of telling your stockbroker — the professional — where he should go to buy a particular share for you. So much the better. It should. And you are beginning to understand that warnings about the speculative nature of this market are no joke. You are entering relatively unexplored territory — certainly for the traditional broker — but that is part of the reason for going there. The opportunities are so much more inviting.

Finding a suitable broker is not easy. If you have been trading shares on the market proper, you should already have one. Hopefully, there will be no problem. As the AIM becomes more established, the barriers will fall.

Ideally, the best broker is one recommended by a friend. There is no substitute for the personal touch. Beyond that, the best bet is The Association of Private Client Investment Managers and Stockbrokers. It supplies a directory of private client brokers. Write to APCIMS, 112 Middlesex Street, London E1 7HY (Tel 0171 247 7080).

Then there is ProShare, a body partly backed by the Government, the Stock Exchange, the Bank of England and others to encourage the private investor. It produces many helpful aids to investment, and charges £30 a year for membership. You can contact it at Library Chambers, 13/14 Basinghall Street, London EC2V 5BQ (Tel 0171 600 0984).

> "Ideally, the best broker is one recommended by a friend"

Share Shops

There is a lot of talk about share shops. In truth, I have never actually seen one on the High Street since the late eighties. Many tend to use the term to refer to people like bank branches or ShareLink, a stockbroking firm which advertises a low-price buying and selling service, plus a variety of extra investment aids, at a price. ShareLink itself is to be recommended for reasonably priced buying and selling facilities, though you have to make your own investment decisions.

Other execution-only services are advertised quite widely, and the *Investors Chronicle* frequently carries a list of them. The Share Centre is to be recommended for low charges for infrequent traders.

Sadly, none of these is a substitute for an old-fashioned broker, who will spare a few moments to chat, swap ideas, and lead you through any problems. Such brokers may cost more than the execution-only houses, but a good one is worth every extra penny. It is foolish to try to save a fiver in dealing costs when bad advice, or the lack of advice, might lead you to lose several hundreds of pounds in a poor investment.

If the share shops are operated by some firm of investment advisers, not a member of the Stock Exchange, tread cautiously. They may be perfectly sound. But some lead you in gently, then may begin to try to sell you shares which may not always prove satisfactory. Unless you are sure you know who is behind the firm, and know that they have years of experience and impeccable connections, steer clear.

Regional Brokers

The distinction between who does what, and who belongs to what organisation, is confusing to the outsider, no matter what the regulators may pretend. Always err on the side of caution. If in doubt, keep out. But do not let my reservations about share shops put you off dealing with bona fide Stock Exchange members who may have easily accessible offices — sort of share shops — on the High Street in towns outside London.

A good local broker can be first-class. Because they are outside London, and may have avoided expensive office overheads and extra staff costs, regional brokers can often spare more time for private clients, and may also charge less.

Crucially, they are available for you to pop in for a chat from time to time. There is a prospect of developing a real relationship which can be of value to both sides. A good local broker might have better knowledge of companies in the area. Hopefully as the AIM develops, such brokers will be sponsoring issues of shares in promising local companies. This could give you a real advantage, the opportunity of getting in on issues which may not be available more widely. Such a service could develop most rapidly in Scotland.

Newspaper Share Deals

Several national newspapers have done deals with execution-only houses, offering low-cost share trading facilities. Steer clear. Most of these will not extend to AIM. But, whatever you want to buy or sell, the service is unsatisfactory. I have refused to allow the *Daily Mail* to become involved. Most such systems reserve the right to hold your shares a while, until they have a larger batch, and can then deal in one larger lot. That means the price could move against you while the deal is waiting to be done. It makes a few bob for the newspaper concerned, and provides a poor service for readers.

Banks And Building Societies

The banks and building societies are gradually getting better at the share game. Many have separate stockbroking businesses of their own. Others use well-established firms. On the whole, though, it is hard to see their providing the kind of close, helpful support you really need. And you may find that most of them shy away from the AIM and the OFEX. Their strongest selling point is security. They will not run off with your money or go bust in the middle of a deal. If they do make a mistake, they should eventually make sure that you are not out of pocket.

Investment Advisers

Sadly, you could end up broke if you become involved with the wrong sort of independent investment adviser. It is extremely difficult to be fair about this. We now have such a maze of regulators, spinning regulations which are often petty and tedious in the extreme, that it is tempting to ignore the lot of them. It is impossible to keep abreast of who does what, and who stops what while at the same time working to earn a living.

In the end, the clever crooks get away with it, at least for a while. The safest approach is to be wary of anyone offering investment advice, unless they are a member of the Stock Exchange, though someone like Hargreaves Lansdown is perfectly acceptable.

In particular, beware of anyone who phones to try to sell you shares. They may have got your name and number because you have responded to an advertisement offering a free investment magazine, a review of a particular market, or even a detailed review of the prospects for a particular share you hold. This last trick is particularly tempting. Sometimes they buy a list of shareholders in small quoted companies, and write offering a research note on those companies. If you accept, you are hooked. They may try to sell you shares in other companies, offering all sorts of special bargains. Do not get caught.

It is hard to be specific, because the hustlers are adaptable. No sooner is one loophole blocked, one selling trick spotted, than they find a different one. Because you have bought a share on the AIM, you could be marked out as a mug. You have demonstrated a readiness to play the high-risk investment game.

Conmen love share speculators. They might even invent a whole company to cater for you and those like you, printing fictitious share certificates. It happens, believe me. Especially with any salesman who phones from abroad, or tries to sell shares in a company with an overseas base. He will be wonderfully persistent, friendly, and pretty convincing. It makes sense that he should wish to do you a special deal, making sure you make money first time out, because he knows you will deal again, and he wants you as a client. That familiar line has hooked many a sucker. Sometimes, he does appear to make you a profit first time, the better to hook you more securely next time. Or the time after.

You may be offered shares listed on the London market. Or on the AIM or OFEX. They may appear a real bargain, priced below the market level. Investment advisers often buy large lines of stock in particular companies, paying well below the quoted price because they are buying in quantity. They split the block into smaller units, and try to sell them to individuals at the market price, or perhaps just below, making a turn as they go. This might appear reasonable enough. It can be, if the company concerned is sound. But the interests of the client — you — are normally secondary. The salesman simply wants to shift the shares at a profit, and will normally be on a substantial commission to do it.

If you are tempted, perhaps by a new issue they are floating — usually the salesman will tell you he is in the happy position of letting you have just the last few shares and will be able almost to guarantee a substantial profit when deals start in a week or two — ask for a prospectus before committing yourself. Make sure it is a prospectus. If you simply get a glossy brochure, describing what the company does, and perhaps a batch of encouraging press cuttings, beware. This may not even be a proper public company. It may simply be a scam, built around some non-existent project. You will never see your cash again.

Excuse me if that sounds over-dramatic. Most share issues, and most share salesmen are straight enough. Not every issue will succeed, but they are legitimate projects. You may never come across anything dubious. But the warnings are worth heeding. Share crooks and conmen are ruthless, and elusive. They usually leave the authorities standing. Once snared, unsophisticated investors have little chance. Through the years, I have seen many of these rackets, and they cause great misery to a small minority of investors. So bear with me through these cautionary tales. I would hate any reader to get caught.

Make it simple. Never buy an investment product from anyone who approaches you by phone, unless you have first asked him to ring. Never break that rule, no matter how persuasive and persistent he may be. And never, ever, deal with anyone who is based outside this country. He is only after your money.

The Policemen

If you do get caught, you may find that seeking redress causes great frustration. Writing this section of the book causes me great frustration. For more than 30 years, I have warned readers about share scams, and so on. While I have managed to give some very successful recommendations to buy, I suspect that my greatest service has been in helping to warn people off dud schemes, and getting some crooks put out of business. Yet to this very day, I cannot sort out who does what among the investment policemen.

As I write, something called the Personal Investment Authority (0171 538 8860) appears to have assumed overall power. Goodness knows if it will achieve anything. Perhaps it will prevent the muddle which so often has had me ringing one regulator, only to be referred to another, who refers me to a third, or back to where I started.

As a member of the public, you might find it helps to ring the Department of Trade, and to ask questions there. As a member of the press, I have found the DTI generally unhelpful and ill-informed. But you never know.

By the time you read this, it is possible that the regulators will have merged, re-emerged, changed offices, or given up the ghost. Or invented a new name and be in the process of fitting out yet more expensive offices packed with bureaucrats.

There is an Investors' Compensation Scheme which covers the most obvious abuses. It could give you back the first £30,000 of any loss, plus up to 90% of the next £20,000 — so £48,000 out of the first £50,000. That covers you if your stockbroker goes bust, breaks the rules, or runs off with your money. It can take ages before it pays out.

If you should get into trouble, try the Personal Investment Authority. Ring directory enquiries for the number. Or perhaps the Securities and Investments Board, Gavrelle House, 2-14 Bunhill Row, London EC1Y 8RA (0171 638 1240). Or you might be lucky with the Securities Institute, Centurion House, 24 Monument Street, London EC3R 8AJ (0171 626 3191).

Do not worry if you ring the wrong place. They will pass the buck swiftly, and tell you to ring someone else. Keep trying.

It makes sense to check if the people you are dealing with are properly authorised. At the time of writing, the Securities and Investments Board were still running a central register on 0171 929 3652. That should give you basic information, free of charge. Try telling them what you have been offered, too. They may not be able to help. But you never know.

The Paperwork

Whoever you end up using to buy and sell for you, if you are trading on the AIM, the paperwork should be roughly the same. These days, you will have to complete and return a client agreement form, giving your broker all manner of details about your financial position. Some of these forms may appear unduly intrusive, and your broker may be happy for you to leave some questions unanswered. Do not be too offended, however. Legally, brokers are required to know their client, and have some idea of their client's investment aims and financial standing. That should help your broker avoid putting you into unsuitable investments. In practice, of course, instead of helping you, the purpose is rather more concerned with covering the broker against legal action if anything goes wrong.

Never mind. It makes sense to give your broker an idea of what you are trying to do. If you have only a limited amount of capital, and want to play the high-risk game, it is sensible that you both know what you are doing.

In the summer of 1994, the Stock Exchange gave up the old system under which all bills were settled after the end of a two-week account period. The plan is to move from a system where all bills are settled 10 days after the day on which a transaction takes place (T plus 10) to settling bills five days after the transaction (T plus 5), and then T plus 3. This is called rolling settlement. It means that everyone has to be fairly prompt in replying to letters, and sending cheques. If you do not pay by settlement day — five or ten days after dealing — your broker could charge you interest.

If you are a regular investor, some brokers will try to persuade you to deposit money with them — it will be held in a separate, interest-earning account — to make life run smoothly.

Nominee Accounts

Most will try to persuade you to trade through a nominee account. This means that any shares you buy or sell will not be registered in your name, but in the name of the broker's nominee account. It makes the paperwork easier, and should help after the Exchange switched to a system called CREST, doing away with share certificates, in the summer of 1996.

Sadly, it means that unless you take special measures, you will not be sent the documents issued by the companies in which you hold shares. You will not get a report and accounts, or other important documents, and will not normally be able to attend annual meetings and such, unless you make arrangements with your broker. Or perhaps pay an extra charge.

This is clearly unsatisfactory, and unacceptable to the active investor. You want to know everything you can about your company. It may be possible to continue to register shares in your own name, and get what you want. Once again, though, your broker might charge extra. The whole system has been devised to suit big investors, and though the authorities are trying to devise ways of preserving the rights of small shareholders, they are in a muddle. Discuss this with your broker. It is possible that some sensible alternative will be devised eventually. If not, it will be up to you to find a broker who will preserve your rights without undue extra cost.

Contract Notes

Whether you deal in your own name, or through a nominee account, you will be sent a contract note specifying what shares you have bought and giving details of the cost. It will normally arrive the day after you have dealt. Keep it. You may need it for your capital gains tax return for the Inland Revenue. It effectively gives you title to the shares until you are sent a share certificate by the registrar to the company. The share certificate — if you insist on one — should normally arrive within two months of the deal, though you will not get one if you trade in a nominee account.

Your contract note will show the cost of the shares, a small amount for transfer stamp (if you have bought), and the commission charged by your broker.

The Cost

You should establish what commission your broker will charge before you start dealing. It varies. Some execution-only brokers will charge as little as £9 a deal, maybe less in some circumstances. Other brokers will charge a minimum of £20, £25, even £30. But they should be giving you a full service, available for comments on what you plan to buy or sell. A good broker is worth his commission. He will look after your interests, alerting you if there should be any sudden change in the market mood, or unexpected developments on a share which you hold. He may charge you £10 or £20 a time more than the execution-only house, but could save you hundreds of pounds.

Never hesitate to pay extra if you have a good broker. He can save you a fortune, and eventually you may grow to trust him sufficiently to allow him to deal at his discretion, buying or selling before he can contact you, if he thinks best.

Most important of all, if you trade with one of the broking firms which sponsors AIM issues, you will stand a much better chance of being offered shares in the original placing. That can yield the fattest profit of all. Profit is what it is all about, and to make profits, you have to learn how to pick the winners.

5

What Makes A Winner?

It looks so easy, this share game. There they are each day, prices galore, over 2,000 of them, some moving up, some down. Look in any of the sensible newspapers, and you have a list of the largest gains on the day, and the largest falls. Each gain shows someone has made a decent turn. And there are lots of lesser gains, two or three pence a share, where someone has made a little. Surely it cannot be too difficult to pick one or two of the winners now and again?

That is the wonder of the stockmarket game. There are so many chances. Luck alone, it seems, could be enough. So it could. But luck could just as easily turn against you. It is not enough to buy a share, sit there, and expect patience to be rewarded one day with a useful rise. You might pick the wrong share altogether. It might drift gently down, then slump, and keep on sliding. What goes up often comes down. And what goes down sometimes simply dwindles almost to vanishing point. Looking at prices, and telling yourself that you knew something was good, knew the shares would go up, is a great game of self-deception. Hindsight is marvellous. It makes up your mind brilliantly. While you may have had some insight into what would happen, the reality is that most of the time, you had a half-formed notion. You did not take it too seriously, never thought it through properly, and would never have done anything about it. But when you see that it has developed into something sensible, it is all too easy to convince yourself you knew it all along.

It happens to me time and again. In recent years, since we tumbled out of the European Exchange Rate Mechanism and the way was cleared for a fall in crippling interest rates, I have returned to tipping shares fairly regularly in the *Daily Mail*. It is a tough challenge, one I often feel like giving up because trying to get things right every time is a heavy responsibility. Winners are treated as a routine part of the service, but every now and then I am embarrassed because one of my tips goes badly wrong. I hate losing money for people. It really hurts. But the average is not too awful. I stick at the tipping column because I believe it is a genuine service to readers. And because it makes me concentrate on the business of investment.

Time and again, I examine the merits of various shares, only to discover something which makes me uncomfortable. So I drop them, sometimes creating a real problem over filling the column in good time. Far better, though, to have a space-filling headache than to recommend something which loses people money. Every so often, I decide against one which later turns out to be a winner. That is extremely frustrating. It is hard to accept that it went up in spite of whatever it was that worried me. The risks I saw were overdone. With hindsight, it is tempting to think that I knew all along that particular share would be a winner.

That would be fooling myself, though. If you imagine you could have picked half of the winners in the price lists each month, you would be fooling yourself too. It is difficult picking winners. There is a great gulf between playing the game in your head, or on paper, and actually coming down to one clear choice, and backing that — either with hard-earned cash or, as in my case, going into print before millions of potential readers.

Why Shares Move

It is hard determining what will actually make a share move up or down. It may appear to have very little to do with what you think will influence prices. Rising or falling profits may play a big part. But not necessarily. Sometimes shares fall after the company reports a handsome rise in dividends and profits. Sometimes they rise on news of hefty losses.

The Weight Of Money

Stripped down to basics, what makes prices move is the weight of money. The more money is spent buying a share, the higher it will rise. The more money investors try to take out by selling, the faster it will fall.

If that appears to be a smart-alec answer, I am sorry. Do not laugh it off as a statement of the obvious. Think about it. The obvious is too easy to overlook in this case.

It comes close to that other old Stock Exchange stand-by — more buyers than sellers. That is a favourite flip, automatic answer to the question of why shares are rising. It is another variation on the weight of money theme. Despite the trite nature of the answer, it is at the heart of what you need to understand to play the stock-market.

It strips away the mystique, the notion that there is something special, something magical, about certain shares, or certain investment experts. There is no intrinsic merit in one particular share, unless people with money believe such merit exists, and put their money behind it.

It is absolutely no good doing a brilliant analysis of some company, establishing beyond any reasonable doubt that it is the most marvellous profit-making machine, unless sufficient other people come to the same conclusion, and buy that share. What pushes prices up is ultimately the weight of buying. If everyone who thinks International Investments is cheap at 100p has already bought it, and everyone who thinks International Investments is dear at 100p has sold, there is no obvious reason for the price to move. It is in perfect balance between buyers and sellers. It only takes one investor to think it cheap, and to try to buy, for the price to go up. Or one to decide it might be best to sell at 100p for the price to go down.

In practice, of course, it is not that simple. The market is much more sophisticated. But underneath it all, it is a mechanism for matching buyers and sellers. Would-be buyers bid up the price until someone will sell, or sellers lower their prices until someone will buy.

It is not the number of buyers which matters. It is the amount of money they have. One big pension fund can usually swing the market more violently than a host of small investors. Now and then, when things are quiet, a string of small deals, perhaps inspired by a tip sheet, can have a dramatic impact, simply because market-makers are opportunists. If they know small investors are on a feeding frenzy, they will try to take advantage, and raise quotations quickly. Relatively small amounts of money may then have a bigger impact. Big money is normally the mover — though, as in most aspects of the investment game, there are exceptions galore.

The Mystery Moves

Hopefully, the weight of money argument is simple common sense. Common sense is an excellent guide to battling through the share jungle. Never let it be said that it provides answers to everything, however. Many share movements may appear to be beyond explanation, complete mystery moves.

For many small investors, that is the only way to view them. There is always an explanation, of course. But it may not make much sense. It may be down to a whim. It may simply be because the market-maker caught a chill on the train coming in that morning, arrived in a gloomy mood, and marked a few prices down because he somehow felt things looked uncertain. He can do that — and sometimes does. He is acting on behalf of his employer, and is charged with making money by trading shares. He does not have to justify what he does, so long as he makes a profit. Or does not lose much more than everyone else when prices are falling.

No rule says that prices only change because someone wants to buy or sell. The market-maker is, in effect, the biggest share gambler of all. He is in business to make money. So if he thinks something is coming to shift the whole market higher or lower, he can raise prices in advance. Or he can change them simply to try to generate interest.

In a lean period, he may start cutting the quotation on shares where he has seen little business for a while. He may know that some gamblers are hanging on, hoping for a profit, and he may hope to scare them out, prompting them to sell to avoid bigger losses, if he pushes the price down. Or he may hope that, if the price is lower, some people will come in to buy. He may be holding a large line of those shares. That costs money. It ties up capital on which his firm pays interest. So, like any shopkeeper with slow-moving goods, there is a temptation to cut prices to try to shift stock.

It may seem unfair. It upsets industrialists and investors alike. If you are running a smallish company which is doing well, and you want to see your share price reflecting that, spreading confidence around, you may be puzzled to see the price begin to slide. There is no real reason, nothing amiss with the business. It may merely be that the market-maker is trying to generate a little business. And hammering your rating in the process.

And so it goes. It may be the coffee price in Brazil, an order from Libya, a strike which cuts production in Siberia — or goodness knows what. Someone may see it as a reason to buy or sell, and you will never find out what it was. Equally likely, of course, it may be that all-purpose villain, the insider. Someone may have found out something which will influence the price, and be trading before anyone else knows. You can never beat that.

It is impossible to get it all right. What everyone is really trying to do is to anticipate what the other investor will be doing next — and getting there first. If you have laid your money down, the money the next buyer puts in may push the price up to your benefit. Share trading is essentially about anticipation. If you think there are reasons which may make others buy, you want to buy first. And vice versa. No one ever gets it right every time. No one ever knows everything, and can spot what is coming next. And even if you can see what is about to happen, you may mistake the impact it has on the price.

Never forget. There are no guarantees in the share game. Whatever they tell you, it is never completely predictable. Many times through the years I have met investors who have been convinced by some clever salesman that they have found an unbreakable pattern. All you have to do is watch for some particular development, the salesman will promise you, and it will lead to a certain profit if you then do what they say. It has always worked, for 20, 30 years. Or some such nonsense. That may even be true. But — I promise you I have seen it time and again — as sure as you stumble in, the mould is broken. The predictable path, the infallible gain, gets lost. And for the first time in 20, 30 years, the unexpected happens. And everyone loses a lot of money. Not necessarily because of crookery or deception. Simply because they believed the game was completely predictable. They find out the hard way that it was not.

Beating The Zero Sum Game

Another of the great market myths is that it is a zero sum game. Super-confident airheads who say this intend to indicate that for every investor who makes money, another loses. In the end, winners are cancelled out by the losers. All the market does is shift cash from one investor to another.

It sounds plausible, and implies that only the really smart

investors win in the end, taking money from the mugs. But it is absolute nonsense. Happily, the stockmarket can generate gains for everyone. Many investors do end up losing all they have put in, and more. But the shrewd player, who picks the right stock, or who sells at the right time, can make an absolute gain, without a loser on the other side.

Industry is all about generating growth. Overall, it succeeds. Put simply, if you buy a share in a small company with a new product, and sit with it while the company and the profits grow, you will make share gains. Even if that company eventually suffers a setback, it will have achieved real growth. The profits have been real, the share gains have been real. It has created a positive gain for the economy. In some fiercely competitive industries, one firm may grow at the expense of another — a zero sum game perhaps. But if, along the way, those competing companies expand the market, they, too, have achieved an absolute gain. There need not necessarily be a counter-balancing loss somewhere else. As the wealth of the nation grows, with value added, share prices reflect that. There will be many ups and downs, but the gains can be real. The stockmarket can and does reflect positive achievements in industry.

What Ought To Make Prices Move

So far, there has been a great deal of warning in this book. The emphasis has been on the dangers and unpredictability of the investment world. All very discouraging. If you have laboured this deep into the book, you deserve some encouragement. While there are no absolute, iron-clad rules, no guaranteed way of spotting stockmarket winners, there are masses of pretty clearly defined rules which influence prices. It pays to learn how the system works, to understand what normally generates share gains — and losses.

It is pretty simple, really. You want to buy shares in a company which is doing well, and is going to continue doing well. A company which generates rising profits will be earning the money with which to pay higher dividends to anyone who buys the shares. In the end, the really big investors who swing the masses of money which determine the overall market mood are seeking a steady stream of rising income. The big investors are the insurance companies and pension funds. They are taking in today's money with a view to paying it out in the future. If they left it sitting doing nothing, inflation would slash its value, and they would not be able to meet future commitments. So they want to secure a source of higher income in the future to cover them against inflation, and preserve the value of their funds.

Dividend Yields

Capital gains are very nice. The dream of making a 50% gain, or even doubling, trebling your money, attracts many small investors into the share game. It should be the driving force for anyone interested in the AIM and OFEX, where many companies are too young to pay dividends. But it is secondary to dividend income in the bigger investment picture. The prospect of a rising stream of dividends is what actually, long term, generates capital growth.

Some shares, of course, score substantial capital gains for years without paying dividends. Biotechnology companies and firms developing new drugs usually make losses for years, spending on research and development. But it is the hope that eventually they will make such fat profits that they will be able to pay a strong stream of dividends that is at the base of their capital growth. Never overlook that.

If there is no dividend, you receive nothing from your investment until you sell it. You may have made a gain, perhaps not. You might have had a share in a terrific asset, but it has been no good to you. Rather like a property company which owns some fancy building built with borrowed money. If no one rents it out, and the company gains no income, it goes bust. The worth of that building to that property company is ultimately determined by how much rent it can earn.

The stream of dividend income ultimately determines the

value of a share. No good having a fabulous mine full of gold which can never be dug out and sold. Sooner or later, production and profits are what count.

So what really matters to a share is the dividends it can pay. Dividends are normally paid from profits. So what you want is a company which is set to earn rising profits from which it can pay rising dividends. The short-hand way of measuring this is the dividend yield, the most common measure of investment value.

The dividend yield is the percentage return from the annual income on a share. Working it out is not difficult. Say you buy 100 shares at £1 each. If you get a dividend of £10 a year, before tax, from an investment which has cost you £100, the yield is

> "What really matters to a share is the dividends it can pay"

10% — a very high return by stockmarket standards. It is more likely that you will have had to pay £2 each for your 100 shares. So you have spent £200 to get £10 in dividends, a yield of 5%.

You can work it out by taking the total dividend, dividing it into total cost, and expressing it as a percentage. In practice, the sum is more complicated, because dividends are paid after the deduction of tax, and you need to add back the tax before doing the sum. Do not worry. You need never work it out yourself. Newspapers carry dividend yields in the share price tables. If you cannot find the one you want, ask your broker. He will get it for you quickly.

As the share price rises, so the dividend yield falls, because you are paying more money to secure the same amount of dividend. Conversely, the yield rises as the share price falls, because you need lay out less cash to buy the right to that dividend. If the dividend is increased, and the share price does not go up, the yield rises — you are getting more dividend for the same money. And vice versa. In practice, all else being equal, a rise in the dividend should bring a rise in the share price. A lower dividend is liable to send the shares down.

In simple terms, the higher the dividend yield, the riskier the market rates the shares. The market is wondering whether profits will fall, and whether the dividend may be cut. But if investors are convinced that a company is set for strong profits growth, and will be able to pay a rising flow of dividends in the future, they are generally prepared to pay more for the shares and accept a lower yield for the time being,

One warning. Most published dividend yields are calculated on the last annual dividend the company has paid. So you see what is called a historic yield. Because the market looks ahead, that may not be so important. Many newspapers will recalculate the yield if the company has already said it will pay a higher, or a lower, dividend for the year ahead. But not all. The yield you see is not always what you get.

The Price-Earnings Ratio

Close behind the dividend yield as the most popular mark of value is the price-earnings ratio. You will stumble over it everywhere under a variety of names — the PE, the PE ratio, or expressed as so many years' earnings, or x times earnings. While dividend yields have a tangible quality — you get a cheque in your bank from a dividend — you never actually get a PE. It is just a handy piece of City shorthand, a simple way of comparing one company's profits with another.

It tells you how many years it would take a company to generate profits enough to equal the current stockmarket value of that company. So a PE of seven means it would take seven years to earn profits equal to the market value of the company.

The detail is trickier. The profits which count are those left after paying interest, tax, and any dividends due on Preference shares, if the company has them. These are often called the net attributable profits. They represent the profits which are available to be paid as dividends to shareholders — not necessarily the actual amount of profits paid in dividends. Most companies pay only a proportion of profits as dividends. They like to tuck some away as reserves against harder times, or to spend in the business.

Those profits are often expressed as earnings per share — widely known as EPS — or sometimes simply called earnings. That is a handy tool, which allows all sorts of companies to be broken down and compared on a similar basis. It does not matter whether the company has 1p nominal shares, or 100p nominal shares. If the earnings are expressed as a percentage of the share capital, the figure can be applied to all different types.

You calculate it by dividing profits after tax and Preference dividends into the number of Ordinary shares in issue. Say a company has one million shares with a nominal value of 100p each, and it makes profits after tax and Preference dividends of £500,000. That company has earned profits equal to 50p for every share — earnings per share of 50p. If you then take the price of the share — say 350p — you divide the earnings into the price (hence price-earnings ratio) and you arrive at seven. So the price-earnings ratio is seven. It would take that company seven years to earn profits equal to the share price. In theory, if the company paid out every penny of qualifying profits each year, you would get your 350p share price back after seven years.

You can do it differently. If you know the market value of the whole company — the value of all the shares it has in issue — you can divide it by the actual amount of the profits to get the PE. Say the value of the company — the market capitalisation as it is called — is £3.5m, and the amount of profits available for distribution to Ordinary shareholders is £500,000. Simply divide £500,000 into £3.5m, and you get seven. It would take seven years for profits to equal the value of the company.

Once again, do not worry if it sounds complicated to work out. You never need to do the sums. Many newspapers carry PE ratios in their price tables. Any broker should be able to tell you instantly. As with the dividend yield, you need to be sure of what you are looking at. Usually, the published figure is based on the last published accounts, so it is a historic figure. Sometimes it is calculated from a forecast, if the company has predicted current year profits. Often stockbrokers base it on a forecast of profits derived from their own research departments to get a prospective PE.

The PE is invaluable as a rough guide to stockmarket merit. A high PE means investors rate the company as having strong growth prospects, and vice versa. Except that a high PE sometimes means the company has hit trouble, and profits have collapsed, though the share price has not yet fallen.

As in everything to do with shares, the obvious explanation is not always the right one. But as you grow more accustomed to using the basic tools, you will understand what allowances you must make. In general, look at PE ratios of comparable companies in the same line of business. If one is wildly out of line, there will almost always be a special reason. If it is modestly out of line, you might have found a bargain — or an overvalued issue. It is rare that the market makes an obvious error. But you might just know better, sometimes, if you have found a company where you are convinced profits will rise or fall more quickly than the market expects.

> "The Price-Earnings ratio is invaluable as a rough guide to stockmarket merit"

Asset Values

Asset values are also important in measuring the worth of a company. It is obvious, really. The more goodies the business owns, the better it should be. In roar-away markets, investors tend to overlook asset backing. But when times become tougher, you appreciate the value of investing in a business which is fit to last through the recession.

Fixed Assets

Assets are the things the business owns. You can find them in the balance sheet published with the annual report and accounts. Nearest the top of the page, you will find fixed assets. Chase them through to the notes in the back of the accounts. Fixed assets are things like land, factories, machinery. But they may not be worth what the figures suggest. Obviously land values vary from place to place. A derelict factory in inner London could be worth a fortune. On the edge of Liverpool, it might be worth practically nothing. It might cost a fortune to clean up the site in Liverpool, and the value of any new building on it might be small. In London, half an acre with a shed or two to clear could be worth half a million — more if the property market is booming.

It is hard to know what is what just by looking through the accounts. Serious professionals trace addresses, snoop around sites, and so on. But few small investors are likely to find that worthwhile. Some fixed assets are obviously of more significance in some companies than others. While a couple of factories may not account for much of an industrial empire's value, hotels are crucial to a hotel or leisure company. A chain of hotels could be worth more than the book value — or a great deal less. It depends on the economy, the market mood, and much else.

Treat plant and machinery harshly. Unless it is brand-new and will not be overtaken by newer, more efficient machines soon, it may well be worth much less than it stands in the company's books. The market for second-hand machinery is poor. So treat fixed asset values warily.

Current Assets

Further down the balance sheet, you find current assets. These include things such as stocks, debtors, tax certificates, cash and investments. Stocks can be tricky. Who wants a warehouse full of Teenage Ninja Turtle T-shirts now? They are virtually worthless. It may be best to knock almost all of the value out of stocks, depending on just how fashion-conscious the company may be. Debtors represent the amount owed by other traders. They should be fairly sound. Tax certificates are as good as cash, provided the company is earning profits on which it pays tax. Investments are awkward. If they are quoted, there should be a note telling you of market value at the balance sheet date. If they are unquoted, who knows?

Liabilities

Liabilities are what a company owes. You must take them into reckoning when looking at assets, because these debts must be knocked off any asset value of the company. Current liabilities are what the company owes and must pay within 12 months. They usually involve debts to other companies it trades with, overdrafts, and the tax bill. Knock current liabilities off current assets, and you get net current assets. The bigger, the better.

Next you add fixed assets to net current assets (or take away net current liabilities), then take away other liabilities. These will usually be loans which may have years to run before they need repaying. What you have left are net assets, or what in theory would be left if the company was closed and all of the bits sold.

Asset Value Per Share

The next part of the balance sheet shows how these assets fit into the company's share structure. The amount of paid-up share capital takes the Ordinary shares at their nominal value. Then come reserves, or the cash left over through the years after meeting the outgoings. Add reserves and share capital, and you have shareholders' funds.

Watch the ratio of shareholders' funds to borrowings. That is known as gearing. The higher the proportion of borrowings to shareholders' funds, the greater the danger. If the ratio is over 50% — borrowings more than half shareholders' funds — look carefully. It is not always a danger sign, but you need to tread carefully. If it gets too high, it shows the company is paying a great deal in interest, leaving less to come through to profits and for re-investment.

Scanning the balance sheet, though, we need to find out how assets relate to the share price. Take shareholders' funds and divide them between the number of shares in issue. If shareholders' funds are, say, £100,000, and there are 50,000 shares in issue, net asset value is £2 a share, in theory.

In practice, you may want to knock something off to reflect doubts about the items we looked at earlier — the factory value, the level of stocks, and such.

Hidden Assets

Not everything which is hidden need be negative. There may be a few assets which are not apparent in the balance sheet at first glance. There is, for example, goodwill. Accounting rules on goodwill seem to change every six months. At this stage, it need not trouble you unduly if you are assessing AIM companies, where such things are normally less significant. But there is a possible plus worth watching for.

Goodwill normally arises when a company pays more than the published asset value for another company. The difference is goodwill. It may not always be a matter of accounting policy. Sometimes you can see the real value of goodwill all around you. The most obvious example is in brand names. Bloggs Bakery may not be a name worth much. But if Rolls-Royce were to make bicycles, the company making those bikes would immediately be worth more than an identical company making similar bikes. The Rolls-Royce name has a magic, a value. That is — quite literally — goodwill. It can be worth a fortune.

So if you stumble across a business with a good name which is being under-exploited, check to see how it fits into the accounting. Someone might buy the company, or part of it, just to be able to slap the name on their product. Or to develop an expanded range of products using the name. Richard Branson is seeking to discover the power of the Virgin name, sticking it on cans of cola. People who would never dream of buying any old cola will try Virgin cola.

Look, too, at the value of investments and overseas assets. Fobel, a penny share company, once bought a stake in a North American door business for a pittance. When that company went public, Fobel's stake was worth millions.

Then there are pension funds. In spite of the Maxwell controversy, there are perfectly valid ways for companies to make money out of pension funds. If they have built up over the years, they could hold investments worth much more than the pensions they will eventually need to pay out, especially if the company has instituted stiff reductions in staffing. The companies cannot simply take the cash. But they can give themselves a pension holiday, which saves them setting cash aside for the pension scheme each year. Sometimes that can make a big difference to profits.

Once again, that is unlikely to be a factor in many AIM companies, which tend to be younger. But keep it in mind — especially if your AIM business is expanding by takeover. You never know what might pop up if your company buys an old-established operation.

6

How To Find
The Ideal AIM stock

Different people want different things out of the stockmarket. Some want a share which will give them a steady ride, no sleepless nights, with a combination of a decent dividend yield and reasonable capital growth. Just defining what that little lot really means could take an age. What looks like a reasonable yield and growth to one investor might seem too little for another.

Something of that nature, though, is what City folk like to project as their ideal, the kind of thing they want you to think they can offer if you give them your money to manage. Older investors will be more inclined to opt for higher and steadily rising income, younger ones will forgo the income, and dream of more capital growth. And so on.

By reading this book, you hardly fit any of the stereotypes. The mere fact that you are considering playing in the AIM or the OFEX marks you out as someone who thinks for yourself, and is inclined to forget the City establishment, and back his own judgement. That can be much more risky.

If you are looking to play the AIM or OFEX, you may be fortunate enough to pick a share which does provide a high and rising return. But that will be a bonus. What you should be looking for is capital growth, the chance of doubling, or trebling, your money in a year or two — or perhaps doing still better. You will appreciate that this means you could pick a few duds along the way. And you will be prepared to lose in order to win.

Market Value

There are some company giants traded on these less conventional markets. Weetabix, as mentioned earlier, is traded on the OFEX. The shares are not traded frequently. But Weetabix is a substantial company, with a market value of over £300m. And in the summer of 1996, the same market still boasted another giant national name in National Parking Corporation, valued at £550m. In 1994, it turned down a massive bid, apparently seeking £900m.

In practice, most AIM and OFEX companies will have a relatively modest market value. They may sell for between £500,000 and £40m, peanuts by City standards. Many big investment houses will not look at anything with a market value of under £250m. They think it is not worth the time. Others are inclined to pat themselves on the back if they are brave enough to play in companies worth under £50m. They reckon they are backing small business.

As a private punter, though, that suits you very well. You are not confused about your investment aims. You simply want to make money. None of this nonsense about doing your duty, or supporting worthy causes. Your wallet is the only cause worth worrying about. It may be riskier playing with small companies — they most certainly do go to the wall more easily than the big boys — but you could make a real killing if you get it right, leaving the big boys behind. As investment guru Jim Slater likes to remark: "Elephants don't gallop". Galloping is very nice. But if you get your AIM investment right, you could be flying.

Small Is Beautiful

Make it a rule. Whenever you consider an AIM or OFEX stock, find out the market value of the whole company. See how many shares of all sorts are in issue, and add up their market value. Maybe you might spare a moment to dream. Traditional City investors will shudder at the thought of buying anything under £20m. You might chuckle at the notion of spotting a stock worth under £2m.

It is a beautiful dream to imagine that company mushrooming, becoming worth £10m. Still a tiddler in City terms, too small for most to consider, that means your value has multiplied five-fold if you first spotted it at £2m. You can afford a lot of losers if you spot one as good as that.

And think again. You know that Marks & Spencer, marvellous company though it is, will rarely double in value in one year, or two years even, unless it has suffered a shock catastrophic fall first. Get your timing right, and you might manage to double your money in Marks in five years. But you will have done jolly well by normal standards.

Your AIM tiddler, worth £2m at first, could double overnight if it gets it right. Assume it was making profits after tax of £200,000 when you found it. It takes only one good deal, one giant order, to double those profits. If it does that, the market rating might rise. So instead of selling on a PE of 10, it gets rated on a PE of 15. The after-tax profits of £400,000 which gave the company a value of £4m on a PE of 10 suddenly mean the company is worth £6m if the PE has gone up to 15.

Sounds good? What if another good deal, or another big order, follows? Profits, after tax, look like rising to £500,000. This spurt of growth could raise the rating still further. If the company looks as if it is going places, it might attract a PE of 20. All of a sudden, the company is valued at £10m, five times the figure you started with.

That may be dismissed as reckless, irresponsible nonsense by traditional City thinking. But it happens. Not quite that way, perhaps. Sometimes more dramatically, sometimes more erratically. More often, not at all. But it can happen with the kind of shares you will find on the AIM and OFEX. And it does.

Small is beautiful. Get it right, and it opens the opportunity for fast, dramatic growth. In normal times, you will not double your money in a market leader. Down among the tiddlers, it could happen. It may be the double-or-bust end of the market. But the chances of doubling among the small companies are much greater than with the big boys.

The Arithmetical Advantage

A £5bn company has to put on another £5bn to double. A £2m company needs another £2m. Common sense tells you which is most likely, though common sense should also warn you that the £2m company is much more likely to go bust.

Consider, though, what you might call the arithmetical advantage — or, if you like, the arithmetical illusion. Let us say you are ready to gamble in the AIM. You invest £1,000. If you double it, you have £2,000, or £1,000 profit. If you get it wrong, and halve your money, you have £500, or a loss of £500. In a rising market for small companies, the chances of doubling your money are much better than halving it.

It is playing with words, of course. Halving is not the same as doubling. I am cheating. But the psychological impact is different. You would be depressed to halve your money, delighted to double it. And if you are going to play the more adventurous markets, you will have to be sensible about selling, about cutting your losses. It is a topic I devote a whole chapter to later in this book. It is a vital one. Unless you are very unlucky, you can opt out when things begin to turn bad. Usually the choice is yours, and you can sell when you choose. So if things go wrong, you ought never be caught with a loss of more than half your money. If it gets that bad, the market is telling you something. It is telling you that you have chosen the wrong share, and should sell. Just as it is telling you to stay aboard a winner, and ride it until it doubles, or beyond.

Where To Find Them

Approaching the AIM and OFEX, then, you will be forewarned. You will know you are taking a gamble, and know you are almost certainly going to buy into a small company with a greater chance than most of going bust — but a better chance of generating outstanding growth. Otherwise you do not want to know.

The biggest problem for beginners is simply knowing where to find such companies. As the AIM and OFEX become better established, the channels of communication will open up. We might see the emergence of more newsletters and screen services devoted to the AIM. Watch for them. Already there is the *AIM Newsletter*, and a monthly version of Newstrack (called *OFX*) to cover the OFEX. And the *Investors Chronicle* carries a special section devoted to AIM and OFEX. Once a month, the *Investors Chronicle* publishes an invaluable list of all AIM shares, their activities, prices, and such. By normal standards, though, there is not a great deal to go on. That is both a problem and an opportunity. Prices will rise most rapidly as more investors wake up to the market. So the biggest killings could come to those who get there first.

The Financial Times

At the time of writing, there is an AIM section in *The Times* on Mondays, but no other newspapers have specific sections covering the AIM. The *Financial Times* and others do carry AIM prices, while the London *Evening Standard* also runs some OFEX prices.

A few of the OFEX prices cover the inevitable football club shares. Do not bother with them. Though some are stuffed with assets, there are often restrictions on dividends and trading, and all sorts of other special factors. Football clubs are almost invariably controlled, and though there are handsome profits when control changes hands, they should generally not be considered by investors out to make capital gains. Luck matters more than judgement for most of them.

You can usually disregard, too, the handful of Channel Islands companies, another specialist area. You will stumble across Le Riches Stores, the Jersey equivalent of Marks & Spencer, and Ann Street Brewery. Plus Guernsey Gas Light. They may be perfectly sound investments. But they are not likely to yield the kind of excitement most AIM or OFEX investors are seeking.

All the price lists do is give you a starting point, a few names to chase. The next step may not be easy, unless you have a sympathetic broker. Ask him to get on to the market-maker, check the current price and size (the number of shares which can be freely bought and sold), and to ask the name of the sponsoring broker.

Most AIM and OFEX companies will have a sponsor in the background. There will normally be a Stock Exchange member firm keeping an eye on things. That firm may have helped the company obtain an AIM presence.

Ring or write to that firm. Contacting a strange broking firm can be difficult. Ask to speak to the corporate finance department, or the analyst who follows the company concerned. Sadly, you might find it difficult to make much progress. Ideally, what you want is a copy of the company's last report and accounts, and any public statements. Or, if you are lucky, a copy of any material produced by the broker's research department.

At the very least, what you want is the address of the company's registered office. There you can contact the company secretary, and ask for information. Most will send you a copy of the most recent report and accounts , and any other published information sent to shareholders. You might even find someone willing to talk to you about what the company does.

Screen Services

Access to a screen service can be invaluable in hunting out AIM and OFEX opportunities. The scene is changing constantly, but most broking offices subscribe to one which will cover AIM and OFEX companies.

All prices are available on a screen service operated by ICV, which reaches many broking offices. Some brokers may not be aware the OFEX information is there. Do not blame them. Keeping up with these things, and the way they change, is not easy. By the time you read this, it may have moved on — though it does appear that each change eventually brings an improved service, if you can track it.

When the Stock Exchange opened the AIM in the summer of 1995, it brought a distinct, dedicated service which is virtually the equivalent to that available for fully listed shares. Most screens carry full notice of prices, recent dealings, and the market-makers' quotes. The Exchange's Regulatory News Service, which covers all company announcements, carries news announcements, and is available to all of the major information suppliers.

Sometimes the market-maker will be the broking firm which sponsored the company by bringing it to the AIM. That may be good news. The ultimate aim for most such companies is to graduate to the full Exchange listing. Their sponsoring broker will be along for the ride, settling for relatively low fees at this stage, dreaming of the day when the company makes it into the big league, and the deals are bigger and the fees and commissions fatter. Consequently, the broking house will be anxious to foster a decent market in the shares, and will make more effort to provide a two-way price. Sometimes the broking house will have prospective buyers waiting to take any shares which come on offer. It may mean that they know better than the seller where the company is going. Never mind. A hint of insider information is a small price to pay for knowing that someone should be there to buy when you wish to sell.

Newstrack

Because the OFEX market is operated outside the Stock Exchange by J.P. Jenkins, there is normally only one market-maker in any OFEX stock — Jenkins. In many cases, however, you will find that OFEX stocks have been sponsored by a broker or a corporate advice firm in obtaining an OFEX quote. Though these sources do not normally make a market in the shares, they are there in the background. If a reasonable broking house is involved, it will come close to providing an extra market behind the OFEX listing. It will often know where buyers and sellers of the stock can be found, and use that knowledge to help Jenkins operate a more liquid market.

OFEX prices are listed on-screen by the Jenkins-controlled Newstrack service. A middle price is listed, with any change on the day, and the volume of shares traded that day. Another page gives the prices at which earlier trades were executed. In addition, there is an excellent series of pages for each individual company. One gives the most recent public announcement from the company, another gives the basic listing information, including directors' names and registered office and registrars. It gives outline financial information, including market value. Altogether, it is an admirable service. If you can persuade your broker to print off the relevant pages from his screen, and fax you a copy, or post it to you, you will have all you need to get started in evaluating an OFEX share.

The Sponsors

Sponsors are crucial to investing in the AIM or OFEX. If you cannot get access to a screen service through your broker, try to persuade him to tell you the names of the AIM market-makers listed on the screen. If there are names other than Jenkins and Winterflood, the market-maker is probably the sponsor. So check with the Stock Exchange or APCIMS for the number or ring directory enquiries, and ask the sponsor for details of the company which interests you. If you get a flea in your ear from the sponsor, avoid that company. It is a warning sign. The sponsor is not playing a proper role in fostering the development of the company. If it is the fault of the sponsor, the company will suffer. But it might just be that something embarrassing has emerged, and the sponsor is no longer quite so keen to be linked with the company. Either way, stay clear.

The Press

Inevitably, press interest in AIM and OFEX companies will be modest and erratic. The businesses are not big enough and the spread of shareholders not wide enough to warrant much attention. Most newspapers have limited City space, and devote it to items which will interest the broadest span of readers. Small companies get overlooked, unless they have a good story to tell. Or unless something has gone spectacularly wrong.

You cannot rely on AIM or OFEX company news being reported anywhere, though AIM is now pretty well covered in the *Financial Times*. At the time of writing, the *Daily Mail* is among the most active commentators, largely because of my interest in these markets. Perhaps the most consistently useful coverage, however, comes from veteran Derek Pain in his regular stockmarket report in the *Independent*. Derek is not a share tipster. Like most market reporters, he tends to report what is going on, without any serious attempt to distinguish between good investment opportunities and bad. He passes on what he hears. But he has an excellent nose for spotting developments in the tiddlers, with AIM and OFEX companies featuring frequently in the insert paragraphs in his reports.

Public Relations People

If you do see a flurry of press stories, it will almost invariably result from the efforts of some public relations people. This is good news, and bad. It means that the company concerned recognises the value of attracting attention, and is seeking to spread the word in the hope of encouraging investors to buy the shares. It is a perfectly valid tactic. No good hiding your light under a bushel, leaving the shares to languish. A decent price allows the company to use the shares to do deals, and perhaps to issue more shares to raise extra cash. It also generates an air of confidence within the business.

If you are already a shareholder, you will be happy to learn what is going on, glad to see efforts to attract new investors and push the price. Be careful, however. It is easy to overdo it. All too often, companies which make the biggest public relations noise turn out to be the ones containing the most hot air. Often the managers are inclined to believe publicity will get them a great deal further than it should. Too much huffing and puffing is a possible sign of weakness. You want the word to get around, but you must guard against it spreading unduly optimistic ideas, and against being pulled in yourself by public relations puffery.

> "All too often, companies which make the biggest public relations noise turn out to be the ones containing the most hot air"

For an outsider to judge how much is too much is obviously difficult. Journalists rarely have sufficient time to investigate properly. They are sometimes inexperienced, and often easy prey for an attractive story. So do not judge a company by the amount of press praise it might get. On the contrary, be suspicious, especially if most of the stories are in the stockmarket report columns. If a batch of bullish stories appears, and the price hardly moves, start worrying. Or if it has a quick run, then settles back and loses most of the gain, be careful. Perhaps the press comment has created the opportunity for those in the know to sell.

If the press reports appear sensible, however, try to discover whether there is a public relations company involved. The company itself might tell you. The newspaper office might. I should not really say this. Journalists hate being telephoned by readers asking questions. They have too little time to help, even if they want to. You would not believe how big a dent it can make in your day if you have to tramp off to the library, find the file, note the names and numbers, then pass them on. All while you have someone pestering you to write something against a deadline. So, please, do not ring me. Try someone else. If a public relations company is involved, ring them. Ask for a copy of any press releases, or to speak to the investor relations executive. You might get lucky and learn the real story.

Newsletters

Already there are signs that the newsletter industry recognises the opportunities on the AIM. The *AIM Newsletter* (0171 771 1390) is run by a former *Daily Telegraph* journalist, Andrew Griffiths. It carries a wealth of valuable information, and does not present itself as a tip sheet.

Newstrack publishes *OFX* (0171 256 8983), which covers the OFEX market. Once again, this is not a tipping vehicle. It simply seeks to report news items from OFEX companies. Sadly it is not widely available, but it can be obtained for a reasonable subscription.

The most eye-catching entrant popped up in November, 1994. Called *Small Company Investor* it was priced at £1.75, and at the time of writing, was off the streets as a result of restrictions imposed by one of the regulators. Hopefully it will return.

Other tip sheets also light upon AIM-style companies from time to time. Too many of them operate in random fashion, however, spraying out items on a vast range of companies without really distinguishing the good from the bad. Tip sheets can be valuable, but use them as a source of ideas to develop yourself, rather than the sole source. And if you are considering subscribing, watch out for special offers. Do not pay the full subscription price.

The Investors Chronicle

Perhaps the most accessible source of information and advice is the *Investors Chronicle*. This weekly magazine is essential reading for any investor, whatever sort of shares he is interested in. It is widely available at newsagents.

The IC offers regular coverage of small companies, including those on the AIM and OFEX, and gives specific tips for such companies. Where these companies send their report and accounts to the press, the IC picks them up and adds them to the basic analytical service towards the back of the magazine. That may give you an idea of many of the investment essentials, from dividend yield to PE ratio, market capitalisation, possibly asset value, plus some indication of how easy it is to trade in the shares. Unfortunately, there is no guarantee that the IC will light upon the companies which interest you. But check it, every week.

Company REFs

Perhaps the most complete record of information about AIM companies (though not OFEX) is Company REFs (Hemmington Scott 0171 278 7769), the investment reference service devised by Jim Slater. In the middle of 1996, it started a section devoted to AIM companies. It carries much of the basic financial information and a lot more and it lists directors, their share stakes, recent comments, profits, and so on. It also gives the name of the broker to the company (not always the sponsor), the ideal source for further information. Company REFs is first-class. You may find it too expensive yourself, but some libraries and brokers will have it.

There is also another way for you to spot potential fledgling market winners — keep your eyes open for the new issues.

7

New Issue Opportunities

If there is an easy way to climb aboard an AIM or OFEX winner, it comes with the initial flotation. The new issue game, which has paid for many a family holiday since the Government set the privatisation gravy train rolling, works all of the way down to the smallest companies. Get in at the beginning, and the balance between risk and reward is weighted most heavily in your favour.

I should know. I have done it. In the 12 months prior to writing the first edition of this book, I backed five companies which would qualify for the AIM. I had three cracking winners, one where I scraped out just ahead, and another where I have probably lost most of my cash. A year later, some two years after the initial investments, the loser is almost dead, and I sold out of one of the remaining three at more or less double my money. Another had risen more than 30-fold, and the other was up six-fold. More recently, I have moved into a few others which have started well. Perhaps I have been lucky. I chose to duck one issue which looked potentially very exciting, because I did not like the personalities involved. It rose around 50% in five months. Another which worried me because I did not like the business or the people involved rose about 35% in five months. A third, which looked pretty sensible and underpriced, rose modestly in a few months, while a couple I did not like fell modestly. And so on.

There was not one total disaster among the AIM issues in the opening 12 months, though there was one which was teetering. Compare that with the record of flotations with a full listing, and it is brilliant. In the 10 months to September 1994, there were 10 issues which subsequently issued profit warnings and admitted that they would not meet the hopes held out when they came to market. Several others slumped well below their issue prices, and one or two almost halved, even without a profit warning.

Remember all that if anyone starts frowning when you tell them you are playing the AIM. The big boys may pretend to be more respectable and responsible. In fact, they are just better at playing the game. Rothschild, Morgan Grenfell, Robert Fleming, Lazards — almost all the top names in the City each sponsored one 1994 new issue whose forecasts fell apart within months, though 1995 was better. Not one debutante on the 4.2 market — the AIM's predecessor — shared such an indignity in 1994. And all AIM and OFEX issues came through 1995 in one piece. Perhaps when you are playing in the junior league, you cannot afford to get it wrong. One big flop, and you may never get the chance of trying again. Because they do not have tradition, reputation and vast reserves of accumulated cash behind them, the smaller players have to try harder. It would be wrong to overdo it, however. The smaller players may attempt to bend the rules more readily, too.

It is easy to get it wrong, wherever you play in the stockmarket. Privatisations have offered easy killings to a whole generation of investors. Few have gone wrong, and the profits on most have been marvellous. Do not let that mislead you. Privatisations have been under-priced for a variety of reasons, most of them political. You do not get chances like that every time. Seize them when you can. But never take a line from the money you have made in backing state sell-offs, and tell yourself that you have got the hang of this share game. You have not. Privatisations were something special, in every sense of the word.

Easy Winners

At the same time, there is an inbuilt advantage in buying shares through new issues. On the whole, they are designed to provide easy winners. Throughout 1994, too many companies and their advisers got too greedy. Maybe they were more cautious come 1995. But in 1994, they lost sight of the basic rule for successful flotations — leave something for the next player. It happens now and again.

Ideally, new issues should be floated around 10% too cheaply. A successful issue is one which attracts a comfortable over-subscription, say two or three times, then opens at a premium of around 10%. Everybody is left feeling good. The vendors like the feeling that their shares have been given a good welcome by the City, the bank feels happy because it has satisfied both the vendors and the buyers, and the market is pleased because those who wished have been able to sell for a quick profit. Everyone can build on that confidence to shift the price steadily higher, knowing that if the company wants to issue more shares in a year or two, it will have a good reputation.

If an issue opens at a discount, there is grumbling all around. The company directors feel that their advisers have let them down, and those who subscribed for the shares face a loss. Some of the shares will be left with underwriters, the people who agree to buy if the public does not want them all, and they will be looking to sell whenever the price perks up. So the price tends to slip away as everyone loses patience and cuts his losses. Nobody feels good, and the company's chances of doing deals in the future are clouded.

Far better to sell a touch too cheaply. A good issuing house aims to do just that. In normal circumstances, then, the odds are weighted in your favour with a new issue. What is more, you save a few pence by being able to buy from an application form in the paper, without broking commission, if the issue is a straightforward offer for sale. Sadly, however, relatively few new issues are now open to ordinary investors as an offer for sale. Most now come as placings, aimed at the privileged City insiders.

Spotting The Chance

On the AIM and OFEX, the biggest difficulty might be finding out when new issues are coming, knowing how to get sight of the offer for sale document, the prospectus. Because AIM issues are small, there is no advertising campaign, no big promotion. The sponsor, usually a stockbroker, will find subscribers enough from within his own clients. Or might link with one or two other like-minded brokers to spread the issue around.

OFEX issues are even more difficult, and may sometimes appear on the market with virtually no pre-publicity of any sort. Once you find one, contact the advisers involved, and ask to be put on their list for future issues.

Above all, then, you need to know what is on offer, and when. There is no substitute for the press, though you should remind your broker regularly that you are in the market for any promising new issues he may stumble across. Several newspapers run a list of forthcoming new issues. The *Evening Standard* in London has one. So does the *Mail on Sunday*. Sadly, though, some are not even publicised in the press.

Best source of all is that old stand-by the *Investors Chronicle*. All of the lists lump the different issues in together, but the *IC* and the *Mail on Sunday* give the name of the issuing house, and the *IC* normally indicates whether it is an AIM or OFEX issue. ProShare also publishes a reasonably good list of impending issues in the monthly bulletin to members.

As soon as you get wind of one, get your broker to contact the sponsor, asking for an application form and a prospectus. Do not be fussy. If they indicate only a few shares might be available, try anyway. And ask your broker to put your name down for an allotment, if he has to.

An Offer For Sale

Easiest to get hold of are shares in an offer for sale. You check the prospectus, fill in the application form, and send it off with a cheque. There are certain simple basics you must observe. Submit the form and cheque in good time, making sure it gets in before the closing date. Fill in your cheque carefully, crossing it as instructed. Sign it — the most common reason for rejecting applications is that people forget to sign the cheque. And read the instructions to see how many shares you should ask for. It is no good asking for 700 when the form says applications should be for lots of 200. No good applying for 1,200 when it says applications should be for 1,000, and then in multiples of 500.

If you think the issue is likely to be over-subscribed — most AIM issues will be — send an application in your own name, with another in the name of your spouse. That doubles your allotment if you are successful, doubles your chances if there is a ballot giving shares only to the lucky names, and doubles your take if the issue is scaled down.

Do not, though, submit phoney forms in the name of the cat or the goldfish. These days, that is frowned upon. Multiple applications are not always turned away, though they have been made illegal in privatisations. Read the form carefully. If it does not say that multiple applications are banned, or will be rejected, you might be allowed more than one application. The snag is that multiples will usually only be accepted if the issue is under-subscribed. So you may get more shares than you really want in a flop. So do be careful.

Intermediaries Offers

These days, straightforward offers for sale are few, and there are more variations designed to ensure that City firms make more money for themselves — not, of course, that anyone would admit it. One of the new favourites is to float through an offer for sale by intermediaries. This means that you cannot simply apply direct and take your luck. You have to buy through a stockbroker who takes a commission on selling you whatever shares you get. In theory, this is linked to some bureaucratic nonsense about making sure that everyone has the benefit of financial advice before committing themselves. In practice, it generates extra commissions. There is no way round it. If you spot such an issue, contact your broker and ask him to get a copy of the prospectus giving details of the issue. Then ask him to apply on your behalf — the sooner the better.

Placings

The most common way of bringing companies to market now is by a placing. I have lost patience trying to track the excuses for why this is done, and it does not matter. It is certainly cheaper for the company, and the private investor has no option but to accept what the bureaucrats have dictated.

Placings involve the sponsor — normally a stockbroker or merchant bank — allotting the shares to their clients, and to the clients of anyone else they choose. Sometimes it will be impossible even to get a sight of the prospectus. Few will be issued, and the placing may be over and done before you are aware that it is happening. Even if you do find out in time, you may be unlucky. The broker may allot the shares to existing clients, and unless you happen to do business with that firm, you will not get a sniff of it. Sometimes, though, the broking house is too small, and splits the issue with another firm. Or it may make shares available if your broker makes an approach on your behalf. So keep trying.

New Issue Registers

You may find that some shares are made available through some sort of new issue register. I have deliberately made this a trifle vague. There has been a company called the New Issue Register which exists to try to inform subscribers in advance of new issues, and to obtain an allotment of shares for them on a priority basis.

I have had doubts about it, and the ability of those involved to gain access to quality issues. There is a danger that good quality issues will be oversubscribed in the normal way, and any new issue register will get the offer of shares in less attractive flotations. The New Issue Register itself has suffered from that, but has gained access to one or two interesting opportunities.

Because the situation does change, the best advice I can give is to suggest you approach such registers with caution. They may not be worth the subscription fee. But they may improve, and there are signs that more will appear.

ShareLink, which has a first-class reputation, has such a system, though it remains to be seen whether it will extend to AIM issues. Hargreaves Lansdown, Embassy House, Queens Avenue, Clifton, Bristol BS8 1SB, also offers a priority new issue service. It costs £15 a quarter, and is accompanied by a quarterly bulletin and other aids to investment. Once again, it remains to be seen whether it will encompass AIM companies. As with all such services, if they interest you, keep an eye open for cut-price subscription offers.

The Sponsors To Watch

Once you have got into the happy position of spotting a new AIM issue, the most obvious way of deciding whether or not you should try for it is the quality of the sponsor — the firm managing the flotation.

Obviously it is not the only factor. Dud sponsors can stumble across brilliant companies, and vice versa. In fact, in the fledgling markets, you need to take a more relaxed view than with a full listing. In many cases, the big winners may be companies with unconventional or apparently unpromising stories to tell, the kind of businesses which may be turned aside by more traditional City houses. The biggest winners may often be the ones which carry the biggest risks. And since you are playing with AIM, knowing you are venturing into the gambling sector of the market, it is no good being too cautious.

It is difficult to draw the line. That is why no investment advice can guarantee success. In the end, it is up to you and your instinct to follow what you think is best. It would be wrong to suggest you should throw caution to the wind and rush into any issue regardless of the character and history of those involved. But sometimes it takes an unconventional approach to spot the big winners. So while safety first is the clear rule in normal share investment — there are thousands of shares to put your money into, so why ever choose one which worries you? — the AIM game is not quite the same. Experience already tells me to overlook the odd blemish, if all else appears right.

That said, there are obviously different categories of sponsor. Some are more cautious, more careful, than others. Some may verge on the irresponsible, ready to try to float almost anything which appears half-credible and will generate fees for the firm in the process.

Stock Exchange Members

As the market develops, sponsors are emerging from the ranks of accountants and solicitors. Initially, though, most sponsors have been established City investment houses, or Stock Exchange member firms. That is good. It means that we can expect they will impose certain standards on the companies they float, and should stand behind those companies reasonably well. Whatever the problems ill-advised regulations may impose, proper stockbroking firms are generally sound, sensible, and well-intentioned.

Against that background, the best way of judging sponsors is to look at the company they keep. Judge them by the issues they have already done. Everyone is liable to get caught by the odd dud. But over a period, a certain pattern and style begins to emerge. If you spot one winner, the chances of the next one from the same house may be slightly better. Success breeds success. Confidence is vital. So one winning share issue makes investors ready to back the next, helping ensure that it, too, goes well. And as a particular house begins to establish a reputation for doing things well, so better companies tend to go to it to handle their flotations. Less attractive companies get turned away by the more discriminating houses. So one good issue tends to attract another, and vice versa.

Does Size Matter?

It is easy to think that the bigger, more established Stock Exchange firms, perhaps with links to the big merchant banks, will do a better job than the smaller ones. It does not necessarily follow. Bigger firms have greater resources to draw on when evaluating a prospective issue, and can offer the shares to a larger client base, raising the chances that the share will be generously subscribed. But the real talent in such houses will be employed on more important tasks, serving bigger companies generating bigger fees.

A successful new issue will matter more to a smaller firm, and will attract the attentions of the very best individuals in that firm. The relationship between the adviser and the directors of the company being floated may be much closer, and the broker may grow to understand the business he is floating better than some middle-ranking merchant banker, despatched to look at the latest arrival on the conveyor belt, taking a graduate trainee along with him to do the donkey work. So do not worry too much about the size of the sponsor. In the AIM, a good little one may beat a bigger rival.

Do not forget that you may stand more chance of getting shares from a smaller sponsor. The biggest City houses will have hosts of friends to oblige with an allocation of anything which looks good.

The Size Of The Float

Once you have satisfied yourself about the sponsor, check the size of the float. In general, you will find that AIM or OFEX companies are only raising a few million pounds, at the most. Some may be high-technology, start-up companies. Those I discuss in a later chapter. Most will be existing businesses seeking additional capital to expand. Often they will be very young companies, one step away from start-up, but with big ideas.

Do not shy away from those which are raising very modest sums — a few hundred thousand — because they appear too small and too risky. These might just be the most exciting opportunities of all. If you are going in during the early stages, you will expect a larger share of the action than in a more mature company. It may be that the company is raising money to take a half-formed idea to the next stage.

In many issues, you may find the company has developed some sort of system or product which appears to work well, and has been producing a few tens of thousands of pounds in profit. That may not generate enough spare cash to take the business on to bigger things, to expand manufacturing or other facilities. Or perhaps to take on a large order. The cost of financing materials, paying wages, and covering interest bills while a small business fills a substantial order can be crippling. Small companies often over-trade, take on too much business, hoping that they can slog through and make a big profit on extra turnover. Natural optimism prompts them to try it without sufficient capital, and they fail. The kind of companies which are coming to the AIM and OFEX are just those which need risk capital to get them over that hump.

If the market develops properly, there is every prospect that smallish businesses will attempt to tap local investors for that early risk capital. Banks are reluctant to supply it, and venture capital companies are widely derided as being too greedy, seeking effective control of a business in exchange for the funds required. A developing AIM will cover that gap, allowing small business to raise risk capital and bring in investors without surrendering too much. It might be very profitable for all involved. So never spurn the chance of taking a share stake because the company

> "Never spurn the chance of taking a share stake because the company wants a tiny sum"

wants a tiny sum. You may only get the chance of putting in a few hundred pounds but it could be the first of several fund-raising moves as the company grows.

Warrants

Some companies make it clear from the beginning that they will be coming back for more by offering warrants with the initial share issue. These have become fashionable in investment trust flotations, but they are especially attractive with an AIM issue. Warrants are usually offered "free" with the initial shares, usually in the ratio of one warrant for every five shares, or perhaps one for 10. They are not really free, but they attract no specific price in the float, so offer a useful bonus, because they do have a value.

A typical warrant will carry the right to buy one extra share at a set price at some future date. Normally the shares you can buy with warrants are at or above the initial issue price. The right to buy those shares runs for anything up to five years ahead — there is no set rule.

If, say, a company is floated at 100p a share, with one warrant for every five purchased, the warrants may well carry the right to buy one share at 100p at set dates between two and five years ahead. Assume the shares rise to 150p by the first subscription date for the warrants. Because the warrant carries the right to buy at 100p, the warrant itself will be worth 50p. So that "free" warrant is doing nicely. So long as the warrant has not reached the final exercise date (when it will be worthless if it is not exercised and used to buy the shares at 100p) it will be worth more than the notional 50p profit. The extra time left in the right to buy has a value. That varies. But a warrant to buy a share at 100p might be worth, say, 70p if it has a year still to run, even though the underlying share is selling at 150p.

If it all goes wrong, of course, and the shares are selling at, say, 90p, by the time of the final date to subscribe for more shares at 100p each, the warrant will have no value. In the year ahead of expiry, it might trade at a token 1p or 2p, depending on how investors rate the chances of a rise in the underlying shares.

The offer of warrants in a successful company can be a valuable bonus. The "free" warrants, for example, in the IES electronic security company were worth the equivalent of around 750p each inside the first year of issue. Not bad. The profit potential in warrants can be marvellous. So if you see them in an issue, so much the better. But you should also take it as a sign of intent. While warrants in a successful issue can be very rewarding, they also signal that the company realises it may need more capital in the years ahead. When the warrants are exercised, they involve issuing extra shares at the allotted price, thus raising further share capital.

So warrants might indicate that the company is planning to grow fast enough to need yet more cash in a year or two. That is a good sign, though investors should not imagine it is totally without cost. Because the company will be issuing new shares against the warrants, it will be raising the amount of capital which is entitled to share in the profits and dividends. That dilutes the interest of existing investors, especially if they sell the warrants and do not take up the shares themselves.

One further point to watch with warrants. They may give you a rough and ready guide to the way the founders see the company and the share price growing. Some warrants carry the right to buy extra shares at the original issue price, as in the example above. Others carry the right to buy at prices which rise with each passing year. You may have the right to buy at, say, 120p after two years, 130p after three, and 140p after four. That is a modest vote of confidence in the company's prospects, projecting a steadily rising share price. Do not set too much store by it. Warrant exercise prices in a successful company will be conservative. But it is worth turning to the fine print, and examining the detailed rights attached to any warrants which are up for grabs.

While warrants are bundled in as part of the package you get when you apply for shares in the flotation, they are usually traded separately, in their own right, as soon as dealings start. Now and then, the package itself might be traded as a package for the first few weeks.

Usually you can buy or sell the warrants without ever needing to go near the shares themselves. This can offer exciting opportunities, which I discuss at greater length later.

Who Gets What

Crucial in vetting any prospectus is who gets what. It should not be a problem with AIM and OFEX companies. All the money being raised, apart from the costs of the issue, should go straight to the company. You want a business devoted to getting bigger, not one where the board fancy getting out from under their loans, or buying a villa in Spain.

Obviously common sense must be brought to bear on this. Some company prospects can be transformed by repaying bank loans, or other fixed loans in the business, and substituting share capital for them. That wipes out interest payments, freeing money to flow straight through to profits where it can be used to build the business, or pay dividends.

Look askance at any move by existing directors to sell shares, and take money out at this stage. When it all gets bigger, maybe. But not near the beginning, unless there is a very convincing story about the need of an ageing director to take capital, leaving his colleagues to go on building the business.

Who Keeps What

You need, too, to check how much of the company is being offered to new shareholders. There is no set rule, but you do need to be alert. From time to time, the most staggering examples of greed crop up.

Check to see what the market value of the company will be at the issue price, after the new shares have been issued. Then ponder whether new investors are getting a big enough stake. An established company with assets and an established trading background obviously merits more for the directors than a new organisation which is light on tangible assets, and where the board thinks it deserves a big chunk of the company simply for the idea behind it. Sometimes you see investors being asked to put up 80% or 90% of the assets of the company in the form of new cash in return for 30% of the shares. That really is too bad.

It is also important to check whether there are restrictions on what the directors and existing shareholders can do with their shares. You should expect to see an undertaking that they will hold them for at least a year. Two years is better. If there are big investors outside the board, the prospectus should also restrain their dealings. You do not want big holders dumping shares the minute the price starts to motor — or at any time. Such undertakings are particularly important in AIM stocks, because the market may be thin at the best of times. The price will never perform if there is a constant trickle of selling by insiders.

Stakes

Obviously you want the key directors to have a big stake. Their interest then is your interest. In AIM companies, it may be unrealistic to suggest that the board should not have sufficient to control the company, and so be able to shoo away any possible bidder. But you should check who any outside large holders may be. Do not be satisfied with mysterious, unidentified offshore names, or large nominee holdings not obviously connected with the board.

Once again, one of the 1994 issues on the 4.2 market had a 40% plus stakeholder sitting in some offshore company. When I queried it, I was told firmly the holding did not belong to either of two suspicious characters I thought might be involved. It belonged, it appeared, to people connected with the two main directors. Months later, a chance encounter suggested very firmly that they were, indeed, the men behind the mask. And the company had hit problems.

Options

It may be good to see that the main players have set up an option scheme. This will give them the right to more shares in the years ahead, if the company meets performance targets. If those targets are specified, study them. They give you a clue as to what might be expected. Reasonable options — up to 10% of the total capital — are good. They encourage the board to work on building the business for everyone's benefit. Larger amounts are suspicious. They encourage the board to try to inflate figures to reach their option targets.

Pay

Board pay is a matter of common sense. Clearly a modest company making a hundred thousand or two is not going to be able to afford more than a couple of directors earning £60,000 each. Nowadays, three-year contracts are frowned on because they may involve substantial compensation packages. But longer contracts may be a valuable source of security of management to modest, growing companies. Real go-getters will not need such security of tenure because they will be committed to building the business whatever.

Vetting The Directors

Amid all these figures, of course, it is crucial to take a view on the directors. These are the people who will make the company work. A proper prospectus should outline their business experience, give their age (under 27 is suspect, over 57 for the chief executive is suspect, too).

If you can, find out how any previous public companies they were with fared. People rarely change that much. Problems at one company often seem to bring problems at the next.

It is easy to emphasise the negatives. Among the positive elements you want to see evidence of experience in the particular industry your new company is operating in. Hi-tech or biotech, it is crucial that the main players have learned their trade by putting in a few years with some of the big names in that business. Often now you will find you are looking at some experienced chairman, approaching retirement, who has decided to gather together a group of younger players in one particular area, and to gamble on creating something exciting. Sometimes, of course, it is the other way round. The younger directors have recruited an old head from the industry to help direct their efforts, and present an acceptable public face. The older man will be lending his credibility to the others. This appears to be especially prevalent among biotech companies, where judging the merits of projects is especially difficult for the lay investor.

Look, too, to see when the various directors joined the business. As a company moves up towards the stockmarket, it is no bad thing to recruit specialist finance directors and such. But too many new recruits may be questionable.

AIM companies are particularly good, in that all prospectuses must disclose whether the directors have been on the board of any company which has gone bust within the past five years. Look at that section carefully. If you are backing someone who has hit difficulties in the past, you need to be convinced that there was a good reason for his misfortune.

Profit Projections

Clearly any company will need to meet the standard investment yard-sticks we explored earlier. You will look at the dividend yield. In a new issue on the AIM, you might find that there is no yield, because there will be no dividend in the early years. All of the cash will be ploughed into building the business. That is fine. The less outside cash that has to be raised, the fewer the share issues. So that more of the company will be left for the existing shareholders.

In many AIM issues, there will be a price-earnings ratio. It is hard to say what it should be, and tempting to suggest it should be under six or over 40.

That is not as flippant as it may sound. If the company has a solid record — rather like the Furlong Homes issue floated in 1994 by Shore Capital — it should have a PE much lower than the established public company rivals to reflect that it is coming to the AIM, and lacks the substance to make it to the main market. If, on the other hand, it is a relatively new venture, making modest profits but with great growth prospects if all goes well, the PE may be enormous. The implication will be that, soon, the real profits will come through at substantially higher levels. So it makes sense to accept a very high PE right now.

Anything offering a PE in the middle may be trickier to judge. Look at the nearest quoted competition, and judge by that. Always remember to compare like with like. Do not fall into the trap of comparing a prospective PE with an historic one.

Happily, some AIM issues give investors very much more help than main market companies in judging potential value. While main market issues do not give forecasts for more than a short period ahead, perhaps to the end of the year in progress, some AIM and OFEX issues carry illustrative profit projections.

These must be hedged about with all sorts of qualifications, and could go wrong. But they provide a useful idea behind the thinking at the company. Some — the Advanced Media Group issue from S.P. Angel among them — produced startling growth projections, taking earnings in the first full year after flotation up from nil to 18p a share, then to 41p and then 116p a share. Supported by detailed profit balance sheet and cash flow projections for three years ahead, that suggested that the shares were floated on less than one times prospective 1997 earnings.

That means the shares would have been a real bargain, if all had gone to plan. It did not, and though Advanced Media was not a disaster, it proved a disappointment after a couple of years. On the other hand, IES Group carried similar projections, and has gone from strength to strength without actually attaining the high projected profits.

Most such projections are accompanied by a page of general assumptions about the business, and by paragraphs of risk warnings. Even if it all should go astray, it makes an invaluable aid to the prospective investor. And it must concentrate the minds of the company and its advisers in the pre-flotation period wonderfully.

Risk Warnings

The kind of risk warnings which appeared in the Advanced Media document also appeared in many prospectuses for companies coming to the more adventurous markets. Read them, and think. In America, they are used to such warnings, and some of them are ferocious indeed. They sometimes work as a kind of double bluff. The prospective investor is tempted to imagine that if the risks were really so great, no one would put up any money at all. The investor is effectively invited to think there must be a terrific story behind the scenes, known only to the insiders. So the gullible punter might think it smart to leap in, regardless.

Do not fall into that trap in this country. Most of the risk warnings I have seen are pretty sensible, but some still fall short. Eurotunnel has a full market listing. The kind of risk calculations in the early Eurotunnel documents looked fierce, until you realised that they did not calculate the impact if several of the separate factors went wrong together. Even then, though the tunnel did not fall in while they were digging it, no one managed to spot the problems which would make the project such a worry. Even in the summer of 1994, they were still issuing projections which were inadequate within weeks of publication. If all of the might and money behind Eurotunnel can miss setting out the risks adequately, you can bet some AIM and OFEX companies will be able to compile a list of risks which may sound reasonable — and overlook the one crucial factor which will send things tumbling. As usual, there is only one sensible remedy. Use your common sense.

"Risk warnings sometimes work as a kind of double bluff"

Nearly New

Common sense comes in handy, too, in watching the AIM and
OFEX price lists for nearly-new issues. It happens more on OFEX
than AIM, but every now and then a newly quoted stock appears,
and rushes to a hefty premium. Check it. On OFEX especially,
some companies gain a listing with so little advance publicity that
they may be dramatically under-priced. Or the market may be very
short of stock because so few shares have been floated. If they have
gone to a hefty opening premium, there may be more to come.
Those who have been buying are likely to know what they are
doing. They will have found out about the issue, taken a view, then
gone in at a sizeable premium over the issue price. In the summer
of 1996 two small issues opened at more than double the placing
price, and doubled again in the next few days as word got about
that they could be high flyers. One of them, SkyNet, attracted a
storm of contoversy and was soon suspended.

Obviously following such companies involves especially high
risk. But you should be alert to the possibilities. Try to find out the
name of the sponsor, or get someone to scan the Newstrack
information screen for you. You never know. It is worth investigating.

Never Borrow

Once you have done your detective work, and have satisfied
yourself that you have located a sensible new issue, be careful. No
matter how careful you have been, you are playing the risky end of
the market. No matter how good it looks, how tempting, only use
money you can afford to lose. Never, ever, borrow to buy the
shares. Never think you might be able to buy twice as much as you
want, then sell some to take a profit to cover your base cost.
Buying any AIM or OFEX shares is risk enough. Do not play
games with money you may not have. That way lies disaster.

8

The Established Alternatives

Spotting the high flyers when first they come to market might be the easiest route to a killing on the AIM, but it is certainly not the only way. It stands to reason that those big new issue winners only become such super investments because people buy them after the issue, and carry on buying to push the price ahead. So if you missed the flyers on flotation, perhaps you can catch them later.

The newer boys are not the only potential stars on the AIM or OFEX. After a year, AIM was heading towards 200 companies, and carried a quota of established alternatives, companies which had been around a while and were beginning to move into a more exciting phase. Already there were one or two companies which might be ripe for management changes, injecting new life.

In truth, the most exciting emphasis is likely to be on newer companies, or those entering a different stage of development. AIM is different from the main market. Because it is not at the top of the tree, it is a market where most companies are looking up. They have big aspirations. They are not companies which have made it on to the public company scene proper, the Premier League as it were. Many will be using AIM or the OFEX as a means of building the business to win promotion to the full market. When it happens, that almost inevitably brings an uplift to the share price, opening the prospect of a whole new mass of potential buyers becoming aware of the promotion candidate for the first time.

Eliminating The Non-starters

All being well, AIM will become identified as the most dynamic market, the place to spot companies dedicated to moving up in the world. On the main market, there is a great slug of British industry which has been around for ages, and is really going nowhere. No matter that some of them are valued at £1bn or more. You see the same companies churning out roughly the same sort of profits, year in, year out. They may take a tumble in times of recession, then enjoy a relatively strong run as the economy gets moving again. Step back, and you find that many of them have actually been half asleep for a decade or more.

There are none of these on AIM, but a few on the OFEX. Most will have moved into it from the earlier rule 535 and 4.2 markets, companies whose shares change hands occasionally, and who figure on the listings largely as a matter of convenience for the directors. They like to see what they may consider an outside value for the shares — though they can largely determine that value by deciding what they will sell at, what price they will take, and who they might want to buy. It comes in handy for estate valuations and so on.

It is important for potential investors to pick them out, and eliminate them from the list of possible investments. You must sift out the non-starters.

What You Do Not Want

What you do not want are the familiar laggards which sometimes trade on the OFEX. A few have done well, but you should normally forget football clubs, offshore investment funds, Channel Islands companies (names such as Ann Street Brewery, Channel Islands Communications, De Gruchy, Guiton, Guernsey Gas, and Le Riches Stores), utility company loan stocks and preference stocks and railway companies. That may be doing an injustice to one or two possible nifty movers. But they are not what the more adventurous investor really wants.

Nor do you want such names as Weetabix, admirable though the company might be, Newspaper Publishing (the *Independent*), and Littlewoods. There might be a time to pick up one of those big boys as the business takes a turn for the better. But they are unlikely to generate the real excitement.

Spotting The Action

It is easy enough to eliminate some of the more obvious non-starters. But identifying where the action might be is altogether more difficult. If you can, try to get access to a screen listing the prices displayed by the likes of Jenkins, Winterflood and the different sponsors.

Then go into the routine we touched on earlier. Ask your broker about them. Get him to print out a copy of the information on his screen, or get him to tell you who the market-maker is, find out who is sponsoring the company, and the address of the registered office. Contact the sponsors and the company, ask for accounts, any listing documents, and details of any press releases. Then ask for the public relations company, and pester them. They might be able to tell you of any recent press comment, or write-ups in tip sheets or trade magazines. Ask nicely, and they may even send you a photo-copy. Once you have them, you can talk to the tip sheet editor, or the reporter in the trade magazine. It is up to you to decide how much trouble you want to take, how much of a nuisance you want to make of yourself. Most journalists will want to help, but many will not have the time to spare. I can tell you that from experience.

What You Want — The Basics

When you have gathered as much information as you can, what you want to see are sound basics — the kind of tests we explained in earlier chapters. You want to know what the dividend yield is, how the PE ratio compares with the competition, what the assets might be worth, and so on.

Because you are dealing with a small, high-risk company, be flexible. Do not get over-excited if you find a solid company with a yield above the competition, and a PE several points below the big boys. That is what you must expect. Investors are not willing to accord average ratings for a company whose shares may not always be easy to buy or sell, and whose modest size will make it more vulnerable than the competition.

On the other hand, you might expect to swallow a tiny yield — perhaps no dividend at all — and an astronomic PE ratio. Now that, folks, is altogether more interesting. A point or two advantage on the yield and PE is no great shakes. But sky-high ratings for a share hardly anyone has heard of — that is something. That suggests someone knows a whole lot more about what is going on than you do, and is prepared to pay a premium for a piece of it. You want to know why.

The Shell Game

Assets matter as well. Go back and check my earlier comments on examining them. Assets may not be what they seem. They matter among AIM or OFEX companies because they offer a potential base for rebuilding, not by the existing management, but perhaps by a new team who might come in and use the company as a shell. In this end of the market — more OFEX than AIM — if a company is stuffed full of under-exploited assets, that is comforting news. It limits the downside. But it might be a family-controlled business which has sat like that for ages, with a management happy to keep it that way, just marking the odd share trade to keep some sort of price in view for inheritance tax purposes. You can never be sure what might happen, of course. Families change their minds, and different generations take different views. But such companies should not be high on your list. Unless there is a radical change of direction, they are unlikely to generate the dynamic growth which you want.

It is altogether different, however, if it looks as if this sleepy business will be used as a shell. The same thing happens on the main market, of course, and creates some of the most interesting speculative opportunities there. Entrepreneurial managers have sometimes built a business which is too small to make much progress on its own, even though they have big ambitions. So they set about finding a smallish quoted company into which they can inject their business and grow it by using the listed shares as currency with which to take over other companies.

If it works, this can provide a rocket-assisted take-off for those who back the new team from the early stages. Obviously there are all sorts of variations, but the basic sums are fairly simple. Say the new team has a business which is valued at £1m, and which can be sold into a quoted company on a price-earnings ratio of 10 (I am using round figures to make the illustration easy — in fact, they might settle for a lower PE). Let us assume there are tax allowances and past losses, so the company is making £100,000 a year, and paying no tax. There will be 1,000,000 shares in issue, trading at £1 each.

News that a new team with big plans has gone into the public company will encourage buying of the shares. Say it takes them to £2, and a PE ratio of 20. If the team can then spot another business making £100,000 after tax, and persuade the owners to sell for £1m in shares, they only need issue 500,000 new shares. You then have a business making £200,000 after tax, with 1.5m shares in issue, valued at £2 each. You have added a PE of 10 to a PE of 20 in terms of putting the two companies together. You might think you have got a combined business trading on a PE of 15. It is likely, however, that the second deal will have attracted attention from the market. The word will be getting around that this is a share which is delivering action. The new team, the story will go, are good news. And since the shares were selling on a PE of 20 ahead of the first acquisition, now they have delivered one deal, and look like doing more, they might well go back up to a PE of 20. A PE of 20 means the whole business is valued at £4m (earnings of £200,000 multiplied by 20). Suddenly there is an extra £1m of value in the share price. A business that has issued shares worth £3m in deals is rated at £4m.

Not bad. But it could get better. Supporters will wish to believe the new managers can achieve something positive by putting together two companies, each making £100,000. Why do it if they cannot improve them? So friendly brokers may be encouraged to feel that the two companies together can make cost savings — something as simple as closing one of the head offices, and instituting joint buying of raw materials — and together can make not £200,000, but £250,000. And that £250,000 must be worth a PE ratio of 20. Multiply £250,000 by 20, and you suddenly have a company valued not at £3m, nor at £4m, but at £5m. Hey presto! We have created an additional £2m of value. Wonderful.

A modest word of caution should intrude at this point. The shares, which started at £1, have not gone up quite so sharply as the value of the whole company, which has gone from £1m to £5m in market value. Along the way, doing the second deal, there was an issue of 500,000 new shares (the £1m purchase for shares at £2 each). So there are now 1,500,000 shares in issue, not 1,000,000. Keeping the £5m total value in view, the price of shares will have gone from £1 to £3.33. The note of caution, then, is modest enough. Early investors have not quintupled their money, just trebled it and more.

Enhancing Earnings

Once started, the new team will be expected to keep doing deals, keep multiplying the size of the company, and the share price. It becomes self-generating. The higher the rating of the shares, the less it costs in paper to buy an extra business. So if you can succeed in buying companies on a PE rating lower than that attached to the shares, the bonanza can roll on. Each new acquisition is called earnings enhancing. By using highly rated paper to buy profitable companies on a lower rating, you are enhancing the earnings of the company at the centre. That is the shell game, par excellence. And pretty excellent it can be, too, while it is running.

> "Common sense will tell you that earnings enhancing cannot go on forever. But while it lasts, it can be brilliant"

Common sense will tell you it cannot go on forever. But while it lasts, it can be brilliant. The smaller the base at the beginning, the better. That is why watching for shell companies on the smaller markets can be so rewarding. Because they start so small, you should be getting in at the early stages, before the wagon is rolling too fast.

While most of the shell opportunities will be OFEX traded, there will be some on the AIM. It is too early yet to have too many AIM duds ready to be rebuilt, but one or two new AIM issues are cropping up with the intention of playing the shell game. They may be smallish businesses backed by big-name investors. Why should they bother with tiddlers? Perhaps because their names and reputations can help the shares move ahead quickly, giving them highly valued paper with which to buy other businesses. Watch them go.

Debt

The more assets in a shell company, the better. Obviously any new team wants the maximum value possible when it starts. It may not wish to keep the assets in the original company. But they can be sold, providing more cash to keep the momentum going.

In practice, you rarely find that companies change hands for less than their assets are really worth. The owners normally want to sell for asset value, plus a premium for control. A shell company has a value. When you come to trying to assess the real worth of any particular business, you may find the most important item is the level of debt. Companies may have assets which are difficult to turn quickly into cash, or may have assets encumbered by a raft of debt.

You need to examine the negatives very carefully. Prospective management teams may be content to start without a bank of assets, but they will rarely be happy to start with a large slug of debt around their necks. So look hard at the balance sheet, and watch for loan stocks and Preference shares. In particular, you might find that Cumulative loan stocks could be a problem. Cumulative means that if the dividend or interest on the stock has not been paid, it accumulates as a liability. Overdue amounts have to be cleared before any dividends are paid on the Ordinary shares. This could mean that any capital reconstruction will be weighted heavily in favour of the loan stockholders, rather than the Ordinary shares.

Share Stakes

You can comb the lists, spot your suitable shell — small, clear of nasty debt, and preferably with a few assets — buy the shares, and sit and wait. That takes a lot of hard detective work and patience, with no guarantee of reward. Or you can swing the odds your way by watching for share stakes changing hands.

The new team has to buy in at some stage. These days, any stake of 3% or more has to be declared. By the time you spot it, the shares will almost certainly have moved up quite sharply. Either someone will have realised that the buying is in progress, or it will have been announced on the screen service before you saw it or it reached the press, and the boys in the City will have moved in to buy. Or, most likely of all, there will have been a solid spell of insider trading, buying by those who knew what was about to happen, or got wind of it between the actual deal and the announcement to the wider world.

Too bad that you will not be in first. But if you are playing the AIM or the OFEX, it may well not be too late. Big investors tend not to follow events at the small end of the company game too closely. Unfamiliar names sometimes get overlooked. And if there is to be action on the shell front, there will be plenty of exposure to bring in new investors later.

The drill is elementary common sense. When you see any share stake, large or small, change hands on a tiny company, try to check who has been buying, what their background may be, and who the supporters are. If you can, ask your broker to find out which broking house did the buying. That might give you a clue.

If it transpires that the stake has gone to the fund management arm of one of the big investment houses, that may not be so exciting. They may simply be taking a gamble. But do not lose heart. They will rarely be doing it without a purpose. Almost invariably, they will have been tipped off that things are happening, or about to happen. Some friendly broker will have sold them the idea. Because he will rely on them for business in big-name bread-and-butter stocks, he will want to be doing the fund manager a favour, putting him on to a nice little mover. These things do not always work — sometimes fund managers get stuffed into rubbish by a broker desperate to get a deal started for his own reasons — but normally you can rely on the boys scratching each other's backs.

If the stake has gone to private individuals, that is better. They will normally have bought it for a purpose, with a deal in mind. Find out what you can.

A Second Chance

If you miss the first move, there will almost invariably be a second chance as the action starts. The newcomers will want to clean up the shell, set the finances straight, and get themselves and their pals loaded with the maximum number of shares from the start.

Time and again, you see someone go into a small company and follow it with a capital reconstruction two or three months later. At this point, they do a kitchen sink job. They write off this and that, make provisions for all sorts of possible losses, and demonstrate that the company is in a sorry state, and would be in terrible trouble if investors do not put new money in through a rights issue or some sort of money-raising exercise. In the process, they may well declare such large losses that the shares will tumble, and the new shares being issued will be offered at a fraction of the previous price.

It can sound depressing. In some cases, it comes as a nasty shock, and can land the early investor with a loss. Do not worry too much. The worse they can make it look, the better they will appear when it turns into profit. And the more they write off, the greater the room they create for writing back profits, or sheltering and enhancing what they will make in future. Often, if the new team has sufficient supporters who understand what the game is, the paper they are issuing will trade at a substantial premium to the issue price, and there could be big profits for everyone.

Backing The New Boys

Do not be put off if the new shares are issued well below the earlier market price, which could involve a share suspension. Remember, this is being done to get the new management and friends in with as much stock as possible at as advantageous a price as possible for them.

When the deal is over, and trading in the shares resumes, it will not look so bad. In many cases, investors will be eager to pile in and will push the price of the new shares well up. But if you are there first, you get the benefit of that low price, too, provided you are sure to take up as many of the new shares as you can.

The arithmetic is simple, but easy to overlook when the deal is first announced. Say the shares are trading at 22p ahead of the suspension. Terrible losses are announced, along with a rights issue of three new shares at 10p for every two you own. It might sound grim, new shares at 10p, when you may have bought at 18p and the price ahead of the deal was 22p. It does not matter, so long as you take up the new shares. That changes all of the sums. Work first on the pre-suspension price of 22p. Every two shares, worth 44p (22p multiplied by two) at suspension will have an extra three at 30p (three times 10p). So they become five shares at a cost of 74p (44p plus 30p). That averages the cost for each share, after the issue, down to a fraction under 15p (74p divided by five). So 15p is the base price from which trading is likely to start when the shares return from suspension.

Even if you do not want to buy the extra new shares (you should), they are likely to be worth almost 15p each, and you will be able to sell the right to them for 5p a share profit (the 15p market price minus the 10p issue price). So you have done well.

Go back, though, to your own position, where you bought at 18p. You have two shares which cost 36p, plus three at 10p, so if you take up the offer, you will have five at 66p, or just over 13p each. Not bad, when they are likely to start trading at 15p each, even without any additional premium for the excitement added by the new team and their plans.

There is one extra trick to keep in mind. Increasingly these days, companies are being persuaded by investment advisers that they should not launch rights issues, but should issue new shares by means of an open offer. This means the adviser effectively underwrites the new issue, and will place it all with clients — taking a fat fee, of course. Usually, existing investors are offered the opportunity of taking up some of these shares. It does not come as of right — which is what the rights issue involves. Unless you apply for the extra shares, you will not get any premium which attaches to them when trading starts. So do be ready to apply, to put the extra money up. You can always sell the shares when dealings start if you do not want to commit more cash permanently. If your broker is holding your shares in a nominee company, tell him you want the shares. He will then "protect" you, and make sure you do not miss the chance if you do not get the documents sent to you.

Any new issue may be time to buy if you had not spotted the opportunity earlier. Once again, find out what you can about the new directors, their supporters and City friends. In 1993 and 1994, Luke Johnson, Hugh Osmond and Stephen Hargrave seemed to pop up in one small company after another, cleaning them up, refinancing them, and then popping established businesses in. Everyone did very well, and any hint that they might be behind a deal sent the shares soaring.

Come the middle of 1996, and they and others in the same mould were beginning to pop up in the odd AIM company, and other, less experienced or trustworthy players were edging into OFEX stocks. They include several names from the seventies and eighties. They still have some pulling power. Check the broking houses involved. Some are especially interested in this area, and can introduce powerful backing for any moves from their client list. One winner, remember, may lead to another.

The Deal Documents

If you can, get hold of the documents relating to any deal. The mere names involved may be enough in many cases to spark the action, and to lure you aboard. But the more you learn about what is afoot, the happier you will feel. What you spot may sometimes make the difference between putting cash in or staying out — or prompting you to decide between a possible quick profit or a long haul.

What You Want

What you want to see, above all, is that the directors are putting their own future on the line. If they do well by making the business grow, you will do well. If it goes wrong, and you get hurt, you want it to hurt them a great deal more than it hurts you.

So you need to study how much their shares cost them. It may be spelt out simply, or it may be a little more difficult because they will be taking so many shares nominated as a cash sum. Do the simple sums. Often you will find that they are selling in a business for so many hundreds of thousands of pounds, and are taking that money in the form of shares. Divide the number of shares they are getting into the nominal sum they are being paid so that you understand how much per share they are effectively paying.

If there is a rights issue or open offer, you want to see how many shares they are taking up at the rights price. Study the fine print to see if they are getting any form of discount, perhaps as an underwriting commission. Look to see if there are any option deals.

All of this is important. They will want to be able to sell their shares at a profit eventually. So it matters what they pay. If they are getting them at a cheap rate, that may not be too bad. Spotting such little tricks is a double-edged business. You may not approve of their getting a

> "The secret was to ride with the sharper promoters in the first, say, 18 months while they got the price motoring. Then to sell at the first sign of trouble"

special deal, yet it demonstrates that they have an eye on the main chance — and those are the sort of directors you want in a small company. If they are less concerned about building a big business, and more concerned about making money themselves, it may be frowned upon in the City. But as a private investor unashamedly playing the speculative end of the market, you are not looking for great empires to be built. You, too, are looking for a profit, and the sooner the better.

It may seem a pity not to take a strong moral line, or to pretend to offer clear guide-lines over what is acceptable. But you really ought to use your own common sense, and your own instincts. In the mid-eighties, I turned away from several small companies in disgust. I had seen the game they were trying to play before, in the seventies. And I decided that it was liable to fall apart in the end.

In many cases, I was right. Several small company promotions came unstuck in the late eighties. As a speculative investor, however, I had made a bad mistake. What I had overlooked was that, while the going was good, these sharper promoters succeeded in sending their share prices racing ahead — before the fall. I had missed out on many a fast profit. The secret was to ride with them in the first, say, 18 months while they got the price motoring. Then to sell at the first sign of trouble. It was little satisfaction to tell myself: "I told you so". I would have been far better off getting aboard and taking a quick, early profit. That would have been really smart.

Options

Obviously it feels most comfortable if you can buy in at something close to the price the directors are paying.

But if you do have to pay more, you might get another clue as to what they expect if you examine any option deals.

Nowadays, most directors are not content with being paid once or twice over (basic pay and bonuses are common), but they want a third helping in the form of share options. These allow them to subscribe at some future date for new shares and pay the price ruling at the time of the deal. Sometimes the fine print shows what the company has to achieve to allow them the maximum option take-up — the company will need to beat inflation by 5%, or something similar. Or perhaps, if they are selling a business in, that company will have to make certain profits.

Do make the effort to work out what this involves. You can bet your life that they will pull out all of the stops to meet those targets and secure the option shares — and that by the time they take up those options, they will expect the share price to be much higher than the option exercise level, so they can sell at a profit.

What was it — Everyone has an angle?

9

Spotting More Winners — And Losers

If you cannot leap aboard a bright new AIM or OFEX issue first time around, and fail to spot the prospective shell, never mind. There are other opportunities. Not every new issue roars to a massive premium. Some struggle to win any gain, and can be bought close to the issue price. Yet others may have got off to a great start, and then go to sleep for a few months, awaiting the news which will take them on the next step forward.

By the time you read this book, there will be many exciting new companies which have been trading for months on the AIM or the OFEX. Just because you missed them at the beginning does not mean they are not worth considering later. Because these markets are designed to give smaller companies access to the capital they need for growth, it makes sense to concentrate on more recent issues at the expense of long-established names. Unless they have had an injection of new management, and are being used as something close to the shell companies we discussed earlier, established names are unlikely suddenly to burst into life. The newer boys just might. Concentrate on them.

A Dynamic Market

Most will have come to this market as a stepping-stone to something greater. The best, as we emphasised earlier, will be run by directors who have not sold shares in the initial offer. They are on the market to build profits, for the company and for shareholders. Even if you are paying more than in the initial flotation, shares in such companies may still carry greater promise than shares in businesses which have been around for a while.

You should distinguish between those that have come to AIM as a way of getting some value attached to the shares, and those — hopefully they will soon become a majority — who have come to the minor markets to raise capital to grow the company. The directors have deliberately chosen to operate in these dynamic markets. They will have taken considerable trouble and spent a fair amount of valuable time to do it, knowing that if they do not deliver, their shares will drift aimlessly, and their efforts will have been wasted. Unless they generate growth, they will be ham-strung, unable to muster support to buy other businesses, and unable to realise the capital locked up in their own shares. You have to try to decide whether the share price already recognises the growth and value in the company, or still leaves something to go for.

A Dream Come True

The starting-point is simple. Get whatever information you can from the company, and the sponsor. It is essential to get a sight of the original issue document. It will give you a far better grasp of what the company actually does than anything else. It will be invaluable if it contains any illustrative profit projections.

If there are profit projections, you almost have an advantage over those who backed the original flotation. They may have got in more cheaply, but you could have an extra degree of comfort. At flotation, you can only be guided by the projections, and hope they work. If you are buying a year or so after the issue, or even after just one set of interim results, you can check how accurate they are proving to be. You are not buying blind, gambling on the prospectus. You can test theory against actual performance. That allows you a much better measure of the company's credibility than you are likely to get any other way. Because profit projections do not appear in prospectuses for fully listed companies, this is one unusual area where AIM and OFEX investors get a superior service. You can see whether the dream is coming true.

Judging The Sponsor

And, of course, you have the advantage of being able to discover how much support there was for the original issue. You are not applying in the belief that others will share your view that this is an attractive company, and will rush to send the shares to a premium. You will know what actually happened. Once again, you have the edge. You can judge how the sponsors have done, whether they have been able to generate a continual flow of interest in the company, and whether they have been able to find buyers if a bout of selling has taken place.

The strength of a sponsor can be crucial to any minor market company. Some brokers manage the market much better than others. They help to ensure that it is liquid, with buyers to match sellers at most times. And they keep the company up to the mark, making sure the right announcements appear when they should. Investment is not always about reality. It is about perception. Indifferent companies which are well presented can make more money for investors simply because more people are attracted to them. That pushes the share price higher. You always have to keep this balance between belief and cynicism. The sponsor can be crucial in presenting a company, managing market perceptions.

Do not hesitate to try to talk to the sponsor about any company

143

which catches your eye. His attitude will help you to judge the way the market is run. Is he enthusiastic and helpful? Or, perhaps, is he just going through the motions because the company is paying fees to keep him aboard? It makes a real difference to the prospects for the shares.

Keeping The Market Tight

A useful indicator you may be able to glean from the sponsor is the company's policy on issuing shares. One of the reasons for getting any quotation is to be able to use the shares as currency to buy other businesses. The higher the share price, the more valuable the currency.

That makes sense. While you want to see deals and action, you do not want to see too many shares floating around. There are great dangers in holding shares in a narrow market company, where small sales or purchases may move the price sharply. When shares are going up, you want a tight market. You want the price to rise quickly on any significant buying. That will not happen if the company issues too many shares.

Equally, of course, you do not want to be sitting in a tight market stock when the price starts to fall. Any sale will send the price tumbling quickly. At that point, you will be safer in a business which has issued lots of shares.

Be careful. Try to check what the attitude towards issuing paper may be. The sponsor might give you a clue. Or perhaps the directors themselves, if you get the chance to talk to them.

The Debt Trap

There is one other crucial pointer to success which can be gleaned from any sponsor — the level of borrowing in the business. Never mind what company, if it borrows too much too soon, it will go bust.

Check the balance sheet, talk to the sponsor, ask your broker. Above all, get a grip on borrowings. You may not want your company to raise too much money by issuing shares all over the place. But at least share capital does not have to be repaid. It is genuine risk capital, gone forever if the business hits bad trouble. In a young business, it may effectively cost nothing at the beginning because investors may not expect a dividend.

Borrowing money costs money. That money — interest — must be paid. It comes before profits. If borrowing is too high, profits can be wiped out. If the company is modest, and cannot pay the bank, the bank will not hesitate to put in a receiver to get its money back. Your cash will be lost.

Check how much interest the company will have to pay each year. Check how well that is covered by the cash being generated in the business. Jim Slater's excellent but expensive service of "Really Essential Financial Statistics" provides a handy measure of interest cover and so much else, but does not extend to OFEX companies. He defines interest cover concisely, though, as the ratio of normalised historic profits before interest and tax divided by the annual interest charge. Low or deteriorating interest cover is a clear danger sign.

Watch carefully, and do not be persuaded that your young company is exempt. Because it is new, it is more vulnerable. You want interest cover of three times or more, if you can. If your company is not making profits yet, you will want evidence of cash in the bank, growing sales, or clearly defined capacity to borrow more, without the need to repay in the short term. Heavy overdrafts are especially dangerous, since interest costs rise as interest rates go up. That often happens at the worst possible moment, when the economy is in a bad way, and when cash from sales is more difficult to generate.

High Gearing

We have touched upon gearing previously. It runs alongside interest cover at the heart of any company's financial strength or weakness. It measures roughly what the company owns by comparison with what it owes, or strictly speaking the level of borrowing measured against shareholders' funds. Shareholders' funds are the Ordinary share capital, plus any Preference capital, plus reserves. If you want to take a tougher view, you will knock off the value of any intangible assets. To calculate gearing, take all of the company's borrowings, deduct cash and any other assets which can readily be converted into cash — such as Treasury bills or certificates of deposit — and express them as a percentage of shareholders' funds. Be careful if there are holdings of shares or other securities. They may not be easily saleable at the stated value, so you may want to leave them out of the sum when you calculate net borrowings.

Be careful of any company with gearing of more than 50% unless you have good reason to expect the position will change quickly. If there is a confident expectation of a surge in sales, bringing cash in, that is good. But if you see that big sales are continually being postponed, extra money needs to be invested in refining the product, and borrowings are creeping up, beware.

High gearing, though, need not always be a problem. If things are going well, and getting better, it can be good. Once the company has made enough to cover interest costs, all of the extra comes flowing through to profits. If interest rates fall, that can have a big impact. So, too, can any change which replaces costly overdrafts with cheaper, long-term finance. Or — best of all — if soaring sales allow overdrafts to be wiped out, leaving more to flow to profits.

This may all seem difficult to evaluate. So it is, especially because you will usually be working almost blind. You will probably only have the benefit of the annual balance sheet, a picture of how the company's finances looked on the last day of the trading year. That can be massaged to flatter the position. It may be unsatisfactory, but it is the best you are likely to get. In young companies, cash is crucial. Do try to keep that in mind.

Cash Flow

These days, companies have to give a statement of cash flow in their report and accounts. It identifies the amount of money a company generates each year, after deducting the cash it has to spend. Broadly speaking, it is equivalent to the profits plus depreciation. Jim Slater in *The Zulu Principle* offers valuable insights into using cash flow, but basically it determines how much is available for expanding the company.

New issues coming to the OFEX or AIM sometimes include cash-flow projections in their forecasts. Study them, even if the business you are investing in has been on the market for a year or two already. Once again, you have the valuable opportunity of comparing projections with actual performance. There may be variations, of course. You need to try to establish just why they happened, whether the reasons are good or bad, and make sense.

Checking The Industry

Sadly, solid-looking cash projections, super sponsors and a tight market will not make a big winner if the company is in a dud business. There might be a brief blaze of glory, but it will not be sustainable. Some of the more obvious clues may be found by checking what industry the company operates in. Even finding the world's most profitable housebuilder will give you little chance of a killing in the shares if the whole industry is in the doldrums. It is no good being a lone investment genius. What brings big share profits is when the herd leaps aboard. You want to get there first, but you cannot afford to stand alone for too long.

It may be a matter of spotting the fashionable industry of the moment. That helps generate interest. But it may also spawn a flurry of opportunist issues, second-rate companies leaping on the bandwagon, flogging shares while there is a ready demand for them.

Often the most tempting industries are the most difficult to come to grips with, and carry the highest risks for an outsider. These days it sometimes seems that the less you understand about the industry, the greater the potential — to win or to lose.

High Technology

Some of the most intriguing new companies are in high technology, developing computer software, or perhaps with some biotech dream It is almost impossible to distinguish the good from the bad. Try reading relevant trade magazines, even ringing the journalists whose names are on suitable articles — though do not place too much faith in them. Try phoning the competition.

Be careful about what you hear. There is a natural tendency to raise questions. You may find there is talk about problems from people who appear to know, but who are merely sceptical competitors.

It happens. In the autumn of 1994, I recommended a share called Magnum Power in the *Daily Mail*. It had risen from 35p to 100p in a few months. I had looked at it when the price was 38p, and decided it was too risky for my readership. As a late convert, I was obviously worried when a friend in the small company field warned of unsettling stories about the company, apparently from someone with intimate knowledge. I did what extra research I could, and decided that there was not too much to worry about, fingers-crossed. The shares ran over 140p 10 days later, and my recommendation looked remarkably successful, though obviously speculative.

Finally the anonymous expert rang. We had a long amiable talk. He obviously knew the company. In the end, though, he produced no more than a series of opinions on matters in the prospectus. He had read the fine print and decided that things might not be going too well. He knew nothing special but had frightened others who had not read the prospectus carefully. He was negative. And, after talking to the company, I took a more sanguine view.

There was nothing more than a divergence of opinion. Expressing it, he had unsettled quite an important City player. Only time will tell if he was right. Eighteen months later, Magnum was still going, still hopeful, but the share price was back to below 50p.

The Boffins

Some experienced small company backers shy away from such high-technology companies. They will never give them the benefit of the doubt. The men who run them tend to be boffins, obsessed by what they are doing, and find it difficult to relate to making money and managing a public company responsible to shareholders. It is a real problem. Unless they believe, their product will not be right and they will lack the conviction to carry it through to commercial success. But they become so absorbed, so convinced they are right, that they find it hard to spare the time and patience to deal with people concerned only with raising questions and making profits.

I love them, and sometimes get carried away with their dreams. I have backed businesses which have missed one forecast after another, with the great pay-day always just over the horizon, if only they can raise the next slug of cash. I did it in the eighties with a company called Sempernova, buying shares on the speculative Over-The-Counter market, subscribing to successive fund-raising efforts, and gradually seeing early paper profits vanish. It had a product for prolonging the shelf life of fruit. I met the boffins, who originally developed it at Tate & Lyle, and was convinced it worked. Always, though, the big sales break-through was one step away. In the end, it ran out of money. It went bust, and my investment disappeared with it. To this day, I still think it was a shame that such a brilliant product never made it.

Never Fall In Love

I fell a little bit in love with the idea of Sempernova, a fatal investment move. But distinguishing winners from the glorious dreamers is hard. You have to believe in some of them, or you simply sit on your cash. Only you can decide. Set yourself a kind of stop-loss progress point. Resolve that if they have not made it by a certain time — 18 months, say, or the second fund-raising — you will sell, regardless. You might miss some winners, but you could duck the real losers that way.

When you set your target, remember that almost all of these operations take longer and need more money than first suggested. You really need a very convincing story if you are to give them much leeway. You need to see firm contracts with big names. That, at least, will confirm that the product makes sense. You will never quite know yourself. Then you need to see the big names laying down hard cash. And money flowing in after a specific period — or you have to have a very good reason why not.

A brilliant product does not make a winning investment. It is merely the starting-point. So many fall by the wayside because they are never quite perfected, or they run out of money, or the competition is just too big and may want to stop them succeeding. You need sound finances, tough financial discipline, good marketing, and so much else.

If you get it, you might have a brilliant investment. Safety-first suggests, perhaps, that you should never back such companies. They are the highest-risk counters in a high-risk market. Make up your own mind. You might want to stay clear. But I get tempted, because the dream is so exciting. If it comes true, the rewards can be enormous. And, if it even starts to come true, the business could generate the kind of growth which will see it through any collapse in general market prices. The rating might fall, but because profits are growing so quickly, the share price might not. But be prepared for disappointments and do not invest more than a smallish proportion of your gambling money in such ideas.

Single Product Companies

Similar reservations ought to apply to single product companies. That makes AIM and OFEX businesses particularly tricky, because so many newer ones start out as single product companies. They have an idea, or a successful product, and have come to market to raise money to develop and exploit it.

If you are going to make big money on these fledgling markets, you need to overcome prejudice against such companies. They may make you the biggest profits, if they work. High-technology companies apart, what you want is a business with a new idea and a clearly apparent place in the market. Ideally, you need to be able to understand the product. It will probably have some hi-tech element, applied in a fashion which you can see makes sense. So long as it works, the gamble is not in the product itself, but in pushing it ahead.

You need to look at the potential market, and decide whether it is growing. Look to see whether it is doing business with any established big name. If it is, it could be vulnerable if the business stops — but such a link does tend to suggest that the product probably works. Then you must decide whether the product itself will win a share of that market. Will it be an also-ran, or does it have any special quality which will allow big volume sales, or high profit margins? How vulnerable might it be to changing technology? Check the patent protection — details should be in the flotation document, or the company ought to tell you — and look to see if anyone is taking a real interest in using it. And see how relevant the experience of the management may be.

Market Value

Many of these are intangible elements, difficult to pin down. You may find it hard to make up your mind about any of them. But if there is one hard fact you can understand, it is the market value of the company. We have touched on it elsewhere, and it is vitally important. Your broker, or the sponsor, will be able to tell you quickly how much the company is capitalised at. It is a simple multiple of the number of shares in issue by the share price.

It can be vital. If you are buying shares in a company valued at £5m, it obviously has more scope to rise than one valued at £50m. Investors are not yet expecting too much. That might tell you that the product is not very credible, or it may be that you have stumbled upon it before the pack. Either way, market capitalisation is essential in making up your mind. It may help to consider two of the more interesting recent examples.

Tracker Network

If there was a superstar on the 4.2 market in 1993 and 1994, it was Tracker Network. Broker Williams de Broe placed just over 3m shares at 257p in March 1993. That valued the whole company at just over £13m — a pretty hefty bite. Tracker, though, had an exciting story. It had the rights to a system developed in America for locating stolen vehicles. Out of every 100 stolen, 94 were recovered, usually quickly.

Endorsed by the AA, the Tracker unit sent a signal which police cars could follow right into a garage. The police have agreed to use it, insurance companies offer a discount on cars fitted with it, and the AA is helping to market it. It costs about £199 to fit, plus £61 a year, or £399 if bought outright. The company is headed by Ralph Kanter, who helped start Britannia Security, a burglar alarm company which spent several years on the Stock Exchange before being taken over.

> "With the benefit of hindsight, it is apparent that the peak share price was expecting too much, too soon"

Tracker has the marks of a winner — new technology in a system which is easy to understand, with great potential in a market which everyone can see is expanding. The business plan involved selling 60,000 units in the year. Multiplying the number of units by selling price, it was apparent that there was a sizeable business on the way. Early projections, in fact, had sales exceeding £40m by 1997, with pre-tax profits a staggering £19.5m. Early in 1994, the shares topped £15, and the market value was pushing towards £50m.

To my mind, that always looked vastly overdone. Things rarely go to plan. Talk of the shares hitting £100 — there was, believe me — was sheer rubbish. To do that, the company would have needed to be making that £19.5m profit by 1997, and be ready to move still higher. The whole company would have been valued at more than £300m — and it all hung on one product. Breath-taking.

Late in 1994, Tracker shares were back around £8. Sales were going nicely, but below budget. In the summer of 1996, it was still looking hopeful, but the price was around £7.

With the benefit of hindsight, it is apparent that the peak share price was expecting too much, too soon. Any small investor looking at a start-up company ought to have been questioning whether a market value of £50m early in 1994 before the company had made any significant sales was not well ahead of the game.

IES Group

By contrast, broker S.P. Angel managed a small placing in IES Group in December 1993, issuing 475,000 shares at 110p each, with one warrant for every five. The company was capitalised at £1.1m. The story was of growing demand for electronic security cameras and retail information systems which helped with stock control, and counting the people passing through shops. There was a contract with Dixons, and hopes of a new security product.

The prospectus gave the size of the total security market as £2bn, with an intruder alarm systems market of £615m. Managing director Roy Ricks had worked in the industry and established a security business which was sold to part of BET. He then developed other security products through IES.

The prospectus carried an illustrative profit projection which built on actual sales of £671,000 and profits before tax and interest of £53,000 in 1993. By the year to September 30, 1996, the projection had sales up to £4.9m, and profits of £1.4m before tax and interest.

The shares hit a sizeable opening premium, and early in 1994 the company was capitalised at around £3m with the shares at 270p. In some ways, IES was similar to Tracker. It was making something with a technology base, selling to a clearly defined growth market. What was less apparent was whether it had any really strong individual product, though the link with Dixons was encouraging.

Late in 1994, after a small extra placing of shares and a one-for one-scrip issue, IES was trading at 440p. The market value was around £10m. The trade press had reported favourably on new products, including a more efficient surveillance system and product security tags, and the list of clients had grown to include Texas Homecare, Woolworth and Sainsbury's. Profits for the first trading period as a public company met the illustrative projections. The company had strengthened the client list and spread the range of customers and products. Crucially, the share price was up more than nine-fold (including the warrants), but was just about in touch with reality. While a £10m market value was high, the dreams had not become wildly overblown, so long as the company was meeting future projections. For my money — and I was fortunate enough to back IES at the beginning and as it grew — it had looked a better bet than Tracker.

By the summer of 1996, after more capital changes, IES was poised to move from the OFEX to the AIM. An earlier plan had been abandoned after comment on deals by Ricks in an earlier company involved in sales to Iran. More contracts with impressive names had come through, and the market value was around £50m. Anyone lucky enough to have backed it from the beginning and kept their nerve had seen their stake multiply near 40-fold.

Resource Companies

More and more resource companies are creeping on to AIM and OFEX. I dislike them. It is particularly difficult to come to any sensible conclusion about a business which is mining gold behind the old Iron Curtain, prospecting for oil in the Far East, or scratching at a copper deposit in South America.

First thing to do is to examine the market value and compare it to the cash it is currently making. You will often find it is valued at several million pounds, loses money, and has no terribly tangible asset value — but there is a massive find somewhere out the back of beyond which would multiply the share price 10, 20, even 100-fold, if it comes off.

It hardly needs me to say that the chances are remote. Why would such a tiddler have a piece of such glorious action? Where will it get the money to develop it?

You will be told that the prospect was too small for the big boys to bother with, or that new techniques allow whatever it is to be retrieved at a fraction of the previous cost, so it is now economic. You will be told, too, that some international giant is in the background, and once the bonanza is known to exist, will provide the money required to bring it to market, leaving your tiddler in for a free ride. All very plausible, and possibly good for a strong run in the shares if you are in early enough.

Once in a lifetime, it might work. Let me promise you, we are almost certainly talking about someone else's lifetime, not yours or mine. The drilling results — there are always drilling results, whatever it is they have found — will look truly exciting, now and then. But the next lot will disappoint. Then the next lot. And if there is anything good, the shares will have risen before the announcement, and will fall when the actual news is published, no matter how good it seems.

The ultimate shuddersome combination is an Irish shell company and a prospect in some remote part of what used to be the Soviet Union. If the drilling results ever look really good, the men with machine guns will take over the business . Forget it.

One or two will come good. In the middle of 1996, something called Pan Andean Resources — Irish-based, South American prospecting — looks as if it could be a superstar. The price on AIM has multiplied five-fold in a year. Supporters suggest there is much, much more to come. I hope they are right. A few others also look half-credible.

The difficulty is that the supporters are always able to produce detailed reasons why their one is right. The fact that the real action is across the other side of the world makes it hard to argue against them. And some of these wonderful finds do come right, now and then. Experience suggests that it will end in tears for most people. I was around in the great Aussie mining share bonanza of the late sixties, when even the *Sun* produced a reference book listing all the tiny players, so popular did the punting become. Very few of those shooting stars lasted. A gang of Aussie promoters got rich, and a host of small British investors became poorer.

The Americans

While we are talking about issues to avoid, it seems sensible to mention the Americans and Canadians. When you read this, there may still be very few American or Canadian companies on the OFEX market, or on AIM. I hope it stays that way.

If you come across any, avoid them. Have nothing at all to do with anyone who suggests you put money into them. At the very modest risk of keeping you out of some winners, I suggest this blanket ban as a result of past experience. There have been a few legitimate companies who have floated on our lesser markets in preference to their own. Hardly any have been a success. The benefit of hindsight has shown — if it was not readily apparent at the time — that they came here because the doubts raised in America were all too valid.

The rest are almost invariably being sold by crooks and conmen, out to steal your money. Do not let them do it. No matter what they tell you, this is no idle warning. Please heed it.

Business Expansion Scheme Companies

More promising, but still requiring great care, are Business Expansion Scheme companies. These arise from the Government attempt in the eighties to attract new money into small businesses. They allowed investors to set the cost of buying shares in qualifying companies against income tax, so long as they held for five years. At one point, that meant you could retrieve 60% of your share cost.

Sadly, the majority of the BES companies proved a poor investment. Like so many small, start-up businesses — a lesson here — they did not survive the recession and went bust. Others were based heavily in property, where values slumped.

For the survivors, there has often been a problem of unlocking the cash tied up in BES shares at the end of five years. Several traded intermittently on the 4.2 market. A few have gone to shareholders and suggested that they prolong the life of the company, and set the shares up for regular trading on the AIM or

OFEX, perhaps using them to build into a bigger business. That means that any former BES company has a ready flow of share sellers in the background, waiting to get out. It could be a problem, retarding any advance in the price. Or it could represent an opportunity for new buyers. Property-backed BES businesses may often be trading at well below asset value. They may be embarking upon a course of merging with other BES property businesses, also with assets available, apparently on the cheap. The snag is that they have not been able to unlock a sensible value for their assets so far, and that may continue.

Other BES companies may have established genuine trading operations and be ready to carry on. If you come across them, try to identify the sponsors, and approach them for the latest report and accounts, and any clues as to what is intended. Tread cautiously. Some may be going nowhere. One or two, though, might develop into interesting shell operations.

The AIM Trusts

One of the strengths and weaknesses of the AIM and OFEX companies is that they are poorly researched, and do not attract investment from the big boys. A few of them have begun to wake up. Unit trust groups, desperate for some new gimmick to tempt cash in, have begun to look at smaller companies. Several possible new funds are being debated, but there are two which have been there from the early days — Beacon and Athelney.

Beacon

Rutherford Asset Management, a specialist firm set up by refugees from big boys such as Mercury and GT, launched Beacon Investment Trust in the summer of 1994. The idea was to invest solely in companies traded on the rule 535 market or its successors — OFEX or the AIM. It offers the investor an opportunity of playing small companies with a good spread. In theory, that ought to be safer, while capturing much of the higher reward from this market.

The Beacon boys have placed great emphasis on getting to know the management of the companies they are investing in and checking that the finances are sound. They have generally been wary of start-up companies, and plan to hold for something like a three-year view.

The Beacon initiative is particularly welcome because it increases the exposure of OFEX and AIM companies to the City establishment, and raises their credibility. The injection of new money into the market also helps. Beacon shares are traded freely on the Exchange proper, and offer nervous investors an exposure to the AIM without undue worries about being able to buy and sell.

The trust has issued warrants, adding an extra speculative flavour which I talk about later in this chapter. If Beacon can generate the sort of returns which might be possible in these markets, the warrants may make an interesting gamble. They carry the right to subscribe for Beacon shares at 100p on October 1 in the years from 1995 to 2003, a good long run.

Athelney

Private client stockbroker Dunbar, Boyle & Kingsley launched Athelney Trust in the summer of 1994, aiming at buying into companies capitalised at under £50m, with an emphasis on AIM type stocks. Athelney itself is be traded on AIM. Unfortunately, it attracted only £900,000 to invest, and hardly counts as a significant player.

Warrants

Some of the most stunning gains — and losses — on the stockmarket occur when trading in warrants. These are effectively long-life options, gambling counters which allow you exposure to a particular share without requiring you to pay the full price.

So far, there are few warrants in AIM or OFEX companies. But where there are, they have scored some spectacular successes. A warrant is usually created with an issue of new shares, either on flotation, or some other fund-raising. Investment trusts have issued them regularly in recent years.

A warrant carries the right to buy a share in the underlying company at a specific price at specific future dates. A typical warrant might carry the right to buy one share at the original issue price at between two and five years hence. If the share itself falls in value, the warrant might not be worth anything in the end. But if the underlying share rises, the warrant value can rocket.

It is best illustrated by an example. Go back to IES Group, the electronic security systems company mentioned earlier. It floated at 110p, with one free warrant for every five shares. The warrants carried the right to buy one share at 110p (the issue price) on or before December 31, 1994, or to buy one share at 130p before December 31, 1995, or one at 150p before December 31, 1996.

Originally issued with no notional cash value, the warrants quickly responded to the rise in the Ordinary shares. When they hit 270p, the warrants were around 170p. The price was arrived at by supply and demand, but basically treated the warrant as a cheaper equivalent to the Ordinary shares. Since each share bought by exercising the warrant would cost 110p, the warrants sold at the full price, minus the cost of exercising the warrant — 270p market price, minus 110p exercise price, equals 160p. Because the warrants would not have to be exercised until the end of 1994 — or perhaps until the end of 1996 — there was an extra value, the time value. That was worth 10p — no precise calculation — so the price of the warrants came to be 170p.

Half-way through the year, IES had a one-for-one scrip issue, so all prices were halved, while the quantities doubled. So the IES warrants had the right to subscribe for two shares at 55p by the end of 1994, two at 65p by the end of 1995, and 75p before the end of 1996.

By the summer of 1996, there had been other capital changes. IES shares had risen almost 40-fold to 320p. Work back for capital changes, and their original cost was just over 8p. The warrants were difficult to buy or sell, because there were relatively few in issue and holders were sitting tight. But their price was up to 310p (the market price, minus the cost of exercising the warrant, plus a modest time value). The real original cost of the warrants — issued free of charge — was a notional 1p or so.

Anyone who held IES shares had done very well. Even if you had bought the shares early in 1994, by that December, you would have more than trebled your money. Terrific.

If you had bought the warrants, though, you would have done still better. You would have multiplied your money more than four and a half times — significantly better than the Ordinary investors.

This gearing effect can make warrants so exciting. It has the additional advantage of allowing you to control the same amount of shares for a lower cash investment. In our example, 1,000 shares bought at the beginning of 1994 would have cost £2,700. Buying 1,000 warrants would have cost £1,700. You can either invest less, or gain control of still more shares by spending the same amount on warrants.

Long Run

There are enormously complicated formulae for calculating the notional value of warrants in the main market. Whole books have been written about it. On the OFEX or the AIM, the secret is more simple. When you look at a warrant, you want to pick one in a share which you think is going up (what else?), with a good long run before it expires. Obviously the further ahead the warrant runs before the final exercise date, the greater the chance of a bigger profit. The amount of life left in a warrant obviously has a value — the time value. Clearly, if there is a year to go before the warrant expires, the chance of making money is greater than with a warrant with only three months left to live — all other things being equal.

When they expire, warrants are worthless. If you do not exercise them, and use them to buy an Ordinary share, they simply disappear, and you have lost your money. So if the share price is below the warrant exercise price at the end of the life of the warrant, it will not be worth exercising. It is simply an expensive way of buying the ordinary shares — though if there is only a small loss, you might want to do it, and establish a loss for capital gains purposes.

In the main market, warrant investors also pay serious attention to the volatility of the underlying share. They want a share price which moves sharply in one direction or the other. That obviously sparks changes in the price of the warrant. So warrants in more volatile shares tend to have greater value than those in sleepers. Until the fledgling warrant market becomes more active, however, this is unlikely to matter much.

Wipe-out

It is important to emphasise, though, that warrants add risk to an already high-risk market. Being caught with a worthless warrant when the time value expires is one thing. Being caught with a warrant which halves when the share price falls 20% is quite another — and much more likely.

The gearing element which makes warrants such winners in rising markets can make them killers in a falling market. Take a simple, imaginary example — but one which is all too possible.

Archer Investments has done well. Issued at 50p, the shares are trading at 100p, and the warrants which carry the right to buy the Ordinary shares at 50p between 1996 and 1999 are looking good at 60p each.

One day, whoops. Archer Investments has been playing the derivatives market, and has come a cropper, with heavy losses. The shares fall to 80p, a drop of 20%. Not good. But the warrants move penny for penny down as there is a rush to unload in a fairly narrow market, and the time value gets wiped out completely. The warrants tumble to 30p, where they still carry the right to buy at 50p, so effectively allow buyers to get into the Ordinary shares at 80p, the same as the market price.

The impact on individual bank balances is very different, however. The Ordinary investors have lost 20% (down from 100p to 80p), while the warrant holders have lost 50% (down from 60p to 30p). Oh dear.

Be warned. Warrants can do that. Wipe-out may be just around the corner if something goes wrong. So enjoy playing warrants if you want super-charged rewards — but beware the deadly risks.

Beware, too, of the dealing difficulties in minor company warrants. You might find it hard to buy when prices are rising, but you will surely find it doubly hard — perhaps impossible — to sell when prices are falling.

10

When To Sell — And When To Stay Away

It never ceases to amaze me how few books on investment take selling shares seriously. If they remember at all, many merely dash off a quick couple of paragraphs, and move on. Lunatic.

Selling may be the most vital part of successful investment. At times, I am tempted to tackle it as the first chapter of my investment books. In the end, that seems illogical. No good telling anyone how and when to sell if you have not first told him about buying. But it is hard to overstate how much it matters.

Bitter experience tells me that investors do not like selling shares. Parting with an investment arouses far more emotions than buying it. Through the years, I have learnt that readers are reasonably forgiving if I recommend a share which then goes down. Sensibly, everyone accepts that we all make mistakes. But should I suggest selling a winning share which goes on rising, the letters flow faster and nastier. There is nothing like a

163

decent investment scorned to arouse the passions of a share punter.

Selling, though, is the essential second half of any successful share deal. Nothing counts until you have actually done it. Paper profits are for the birds. All that matters is money in the bank. Never boast how well you are doing until you have taken your profit. The market is always liable to catch you out, prove you a fool. In a rising market, it is relatively easy to pick a share that goes up. (Please note: I did say relatively. Never let anyone tell you it is really easy). It only becomes a winning investment, though, when you get out at a profit.

Cutting Your Losses

Anyone who has read any of my investment books will find all of this familiar. It deserves repeating, hammering home until it is engraved on every investor's heart, and worms a way into his reflexes. The oldest, simplest rule in investment is still the best, the one essential — CUT YOUR LOSSES QUICKLY, AND LET YOUR PROFITS RUN.

Almost everyone has heard it at some time. Almost everyone, it seems, ignores it from time to time. We all get too smart to use our common sense consistently. We end up paying for it — quite literally.

Do not get caught out. Please heed this lesson. Learn to love it and use it all of the time, especially when you are playing the AIM. This book is peppered with warnings about risk in the fledgling markets. It would be irresponsible to write such a book without them. If you are walking on the wild side, it makes sense to be ultra-cautious. Though it may irritate you for a while if you should do it, it is far better to sell a winning share too soon than get caught with a nasty loser. If you have taken a profit, you have the cash to try again. If you have taken a hefty loss, you might be out of the game completely.

Narrow Markets

The biggest danger in the AIM and the OFEX is the narrowness of the market. There will be times when a sale of as few as 500 shares, worth perhaps as little as £250, will wipe 10% off the value of your shares, off the stockmarket price of the whole company. It could happen for the most trivial reason. One investor might need a few pounds to pay for a birthday present. If they sell the wrong share on the wrong day, when the market is looking sticky, and the market-maker is nervous, it could wallop the price way beyond anything which might conceivably seem sensible.

It is no use moaning. It happens. The price is all that counts. And if the price falls 10%, perhaps one or two other nervous investors might sell, and push it down another 10%. The market-maker might imagine something nasty is afoot, might think the sellers know something special. So he might mark the price down by a further 20%, or more. In AIM shares especially, the price could plunge before you can blink, all for no reason.

If you can afford to stay on, if you are convinced all is well, if you know you will not need the money for ages, then it may not matter. Perhaps you can hold on, and perhaps you will see the price recover just as quickly, if a few buyers come in. Maybe all will end well. Maybe not.

The risk is yours. The decision to sit tight or to sell out is yours. The gain or loss will be yours. No good appealing to anyone else.

It takes nerve to invest in the junior markets. The rewards may be marvellous but the risks are high. It makes sense not to make them higher by closing your eyes and refusing to sell if you are on a loser.

The example of a plunging price I have given may be over-dramatic, and improbable. But far from impossible. If you play the AIM, you must try to keep in touch with the price, and you must try to exert some discipline over when you will sell.

As I write this, I have had an order with my broker to sell 500 warrants in an AIM stock. I kept them when I sold the actual shares, at a tidy profit. I got the warrants "free" when I bought the shares as a new issue. On paper, the warrants are worth more than

£500. A while back, I decided I did not like the way the company was moving, so I asked to sell the warrants. So far, the sell order has been with my broker for four months. Though the price on the screen looks good, and I would take less, no one has shown any interest in the warrants. They have hardly traded for months, even though there have been buyers for the Ordinary shares. The amount is small, so it does not matter. But it acts as a warning of what can happen in the AIM, even when times are good.

The whole philosophy of cutting losses quickly and letting profits run makes so much sense. If you make it a rule to sell losers before the loss gets too great, and to sit tight with winners while the profit climbs, you will almost certainly come out ahead, even if you pick only one winner for every loser.

It all depends on when you make your move. A little simple example will show the logic. Say you decide to sell whenever the price falls by 20%. So for each £1,000 investment, you lose £200 on selling, and another, say, £50 in dealing costs. Your £1,000 is down to £750. In normal circumstances, you never lose more. It is your choice.

If you put your £1,000 into a winner, and stay with it, the chances that it will rise by more than £250 are reasonably good. After all, while you are putting an iron-clad limit on your losses, you are leaving the limit on your profits open. You may get five winners, five losers. None of the losers will go down more than £250, because you will sell before they can. But the odds on one of your winners eventually doubling must be good. That will cover all of your losses, even if none of the others rises by more than 20%.

The example is not scientific, of course. But if you follow the advice in this book, and you play the high-risk, high-return AIM, you will be inclined to believe it feels right.

The Stop-loss System

It is a small step from setting yourself a limit on your losses to adopting a fully-fledged stop-loss system. Once again, this features in all my investment books. I have learnt it the hard way. Bob Beckman, that most controversial of investment commentators, told me about it over 25 years ago. It was not new then. Ever since, I have used it extensively when recommending shares, and use it faithfully in my *Daily Mail* share tipping columns.

Truthfully, I disregarded it myself until the 1987 crash. I thought I was too smart, thought I had a feel for the market, and had done my homework on certain shares so thoroughly that I knew better. They could not possibly turn that wrong. I found out the hard way, losing all of the profits I had made in the 1974 crash, and coming a cropper again in a small way in the early eighties. In 1987, I gave my broker stop-loss levels on all of my shares. He sold me out within days. For a while, I cursed myself for selling too soon. Later, I came to see that my stop-loss sales had been brilliant. The shares I first thought I had sold too hastily later went down and down. Had I held on, I would have lost perhaps three-quarters of my cash.

The Opportunity Cost

That would have been bad enough. More important, the cost in terms of lost opportunities would have been much greater. The cash I retrieved in my stop-loss sales served as a stake to get me going again when conditions improved. It sat around doing little for a couple of years. Then I began to dip back into the market again, picked one or two winners, and was able to find some modest resources to play as the fledgling market opportunities began to emerge. Already, I have multiplied that stake many times over. Do not get me wrong. The sums involved were modest. Even now, the stakes are not enormous. But there is now quite serious money involved. Whether I keep it when the market cracks eventually will be determined by how well I succeed in selling and taking my profits.

Setting A Price To Sell

The stop-loss system is very simple, always a virtue. Complex routines are hard to follow, and tend to get abandoned along the way. Start from the very beginning. Whenever you buy a share, set a price at which you will sell, if it should fall. Stick to that price. Never, ever lower it (regular *Daily Mail* readers will know that once or twice in the first two years of my nineties tipping column, I did break my rule, and did lower the selling price. There were special circumstances. Do as I say, not as I do).

It may sound defeatist, setting a selling price which will lose you money. You are only buying because you think you have found a winner, after all. Never mind. Do it. Tell yourself you will not need it, because you have found a winner.

Set your stop-loss price somewhere between 15% and 25% below the price you pay. This is a purely arbitrary limit. You can do it differently, if you choose. Judge where to set the stop-loss by reference to the volatility of the price, the spread between the buying and selling price, and the degree of risk you are ready to take.

Using the stop-loss on fully listed shares, I normally like to set it 10% to 20% below the purchase price, using the middle price. And I shift it closer to the price if I get uneasy about the market mood, or feel the share might be getting overvalued. On the AIM or OFEX, it is probably best to allow yourself more leeway. Most of the shares you will be trading in will be a narrow market, and will be more volatile than the average share. Because they will move more sharply in either direction, you might find the price hits your stop-loss very quickly if you set it too tight.

It is really a matter for your own judgement. There is no set rule. The only rule I would make mandatory is that you do set some sort of stop-loss. Jim Slater in *The Zulu Principle* suggests 25% for growth shares, turn-arounds and cyclicals, and 40% for shells. You might even be prepared to set a 50% limit for AIM and OFEX companies. It is up to you. In practice, I think 40% to 50% is too much leeway.

What The Market Is Telling You

Beckman frequently says: "Listen to what the market is telling you". It makes a lot of sense. You might not always understand what the market is telling you, of course. But if your share has fallen by 25%, the market is probably telling you that you have got it wrong. Remember — the price merely reflects the collective opinion of many investors, some of whom will be insiders who know much more than you do. You never know, of course, when any bout of selling will stop. You might decide to quit at the bottom, just before a rally. Too bad. Better safe than sorry. The market might be telling you that you have picked a real dud, one that is going down to nothing, or pretty near. If that should happen, you will feel pretty smart if you sold with just a 25% loss.

Raising The Stop-loss

We are looking on the gloomy side. Just a precaution, slotting in the stop-loss. With the power of positive thinking, you are going to see your choice move ahead nicely. As it does, you should then raise the stop-loss as the price of your share goes up. Your stop-loss becomes a trailing stop-loss, trailing up behind the share price. Again, the refinement is up to you. Move it up penny for penny behind the price, as it goes. Or you may prefer to watch for a week, see if the price settles at the new higher level, and then move your stop-loss up.

It works nicely. If you bought, say, at 100p, you would set a stop-loss at, say, 80p. If the price falls to 80p, then you sell, no matter what. Never move the stop-loss down. If it goes happily up to 110p, raise the stop-loss to 90p. If it goes to 120p, raise it to 100p. At 150p, your stop-loss should be up to 130p. And so on.

Running Your Profits

The system has the virtue that it makes you run profits and cut losses. You do not need worry about when to sell. The system tells you.

It is not perfect. It does mean that you never sell at the very top. You always sell at 20% below the best, if 20% is your chosen stop-loss margin. But then you never take a loss of more than 20%.

Sometimes it might take you out of a winner far too early — even at a loss. There is no guarantee that a price might not suddenly fall quite sharply, then rally and go on to new peaks. You might be caught out in that sudden sharp fall, sell, and miss a big winner. It happens now and then. No system ever gets it right every time. Hard experience tells me, though, that the risk of losing out on a few winners is well worth taking if it saves you from being slammed by big losers.

Selling Half

Experience, too, suggests that this system is much superior to the common notion that you should sell half of any big winner when it doubles. That way, you have retrieved your original investment, and are left holding the remaining shares for nothing. The risk is eliminated entirely, and you are sitting pretty, playing with your profits. If something goes badly wrong, you have lost nothing.

Superficially appealing, this is poor investment advice in my view. It is hard enough finding a big winner. When you have one, you want to ride it, see it soar all of the way up. Why sell half just as it is getting into its stride? That is no way to play, certainly not in the AIM or OFEX. You are only playing these speculative markets in the hope of a big killing. Otherwise the risk is not worth it. Do not be faint-hearted. The more money you can pile into a big winner, the better.

Take a simple example, one I give in my book *How To Make A Killing In Penny Shares*. If you had put £500 into Polly Peck at 20p in the early eighties, shortly after Asil Nadir bought in, you might have sold half at 40p. How would have felt when it hit 400p? Pretty good, no doubt, because you would have had some shares in a big winner. But if you had kept your full £500 stake, you would have been sitting on shares worth £10,000. If you had sold half at 40p, you would have had £5,500. Not bad, but not nearly so good.

And think how you would have felt if you had held on until Polly topped £30, which it did a couple of years later. Your £500 would have been worth £75,000.

Take it a step further. Polly actually ran all the way up to £36 at around that time. If you had been sitting there, biting your nails, scarcely able to believe your luck, with your stop-loss in place, you would have sold when the price fell just below £29. You would have banked most of that £75,000.

A dream? Perhaps. In fact, you would almost certainly have refined your stop-loss, and moved it up to, say, 10% behind the price. So you might have sold at just over £32, or you might have been stop-lossed out by one of the hiccups on the way up.

Never mind the detail. The message is clear. For all of the later troubles, Polly Peck is an example which really happened. There are others which have done spectacularly well in run-away bull markets, rising 100 times or more. Most fell to earth at some stage. If you ran a trailing stop-loss, though, you might have stayed aboard for the best part of the ride. If you sold half when the price doubled, it would still have been good. But only half as good.

Refining The System

If you get the impression that I am a passionate believer in the stop-loss system, good. I am. Nothing I have come across in more than 30 years in the game makes nearly so much sense. But nothing says you have to be a complete slave to the system. You can refine it to suit your style, tinker at the edges.

If you get nervous about your share, or about the market, reduce the stop-loss margin. Bring the limit close up behind the price. Or if you have a big profit to play with, and feel relaxed about taking a little more risk when the whole market mood grows sour, do not raise the stop-loss behind the price with every move up. So, for example, if you bought at 100p, and the price is 240p, instead of keeping your stop-loss 20p behind the price, when it next moves to 250p, keep the stop-loss at 220p, widening the margin to 30p.

Or operate it on a percentage system. When you began, a stop-loss of 80p against a buying price of 100p gave a fairly generous 20% margin for error. By the time the price is 240p — hallelujah! — a 20% margin would need to have the stop-loss at 192p. If that seems sensible, do it. You are effectively lowering the stop-loss margin, taking more risk, but in circumstances which make sense.

Do it, though, with your eyes open. Understand that you are assuming an extra degree of risk. You are putting more of your profit at risk.

That could be especially important when playing the junior markets. They are more volatile, and it may be more sensible to widen the stop-loss margins. Or, if you grow nervous, to narrow them. I am sorry if it sounds contradictory. No system can be fully automatic. Investors must exercise their own judgement. That is what makes one more successful than the other. Nothing I write in this book can bring any guarantees. All it can do is help make you more aware of the possibilities. And, crucially, try to help ensure that you have a plan, and make your choices knowingly.

Your Broker And The Stop-loss

Sadly, few brokers will operate a stop-loss system for you automatically. You cannot give them your limits, and assume they will follow them for you. Some brokers will try. ShareLink has been talking about instituting such a system, for an extra charge, for some time.

In the end, though, it is up to you. You need to follow prices as closely as you can, and that is not always easy in AIM and OFEX stocks. You might miss the move.

If you do, you should still keep the system alive. If the share has fallen through your stop-loss before you could act, sell it. Do not be tempted to gamble on it bouncing back, giving you an opportunity to sell at a better price. The system is designed precisely to remove such temptations. It supplies a discipline most of us lack. Accept it.

If you get into relatively big money investment, you may find there are automatic systems which follow prices regularly, and bleep you if a price hits a particular point. They are expensive, and require you to carry an electronic card. I suspect that will be too expensive for most readers of this book, though if you do get a big winner, and find you are hanging on to a fat profit, it might be worth considering.

If In Doubt, Sell Out

Time and again, the investment game comes down to simple common sense. No system, however sophisticated, can beat it, though it eludes many in the City much of the time. Common sense should tell you — IF IN DOUBT, SELL OUT.

You are not one of the great City institutional investors, stuffed with cash which you must have in the market if you are doing your job — though it beats me why there is such devotion to the idea that any fund manager is merely doing his job if he sits tight in a market which is obviously falling.

As a private investor, you have a great advantage over the professionals. You are responsible to no one but yourself. If you want to sell, you can. If you try to sell, you probably can. You are unlikely to be holding so many shares that you would wallop the price if you tried to get out. There is little reason for you to stay invested if you have any doubt about the future.

> "As a private investor, you have a great advantage over the professionals. You are responsible to no one but yourself"

Use that freedom. If in doubt, sell out. Why not? You are in the game to make money and to have a little fun. If it becomes a burden, a worry, do not play. Take your money away. Put it in a building society until you feel better.

Would You Buy Now?

Strictly speaking, there is an easy test for your doubts. Try to step away from your favourite share and act as if you had stumbled across it for the first time. Check the dividend yield, the price earnings ratio, the assets, and the prospects against the competition. Then ask yourself if you would buy if you had just found this share for the first time.

If you are not so sure, perhaps you ought not to be holding it. Perhaps you should sell. Do not allow yourself to become romantically involved. You must not fall in love forever with a share. If you no longer find the company attractive, why should other potential investors buy it? After all, the weight of new money coming in is what will push it higher. If you cannot construct a case for putting extra money in, maybe you should take your money out.

That is a tough measure. I find it hard to apply. There is a great temptation to allow your winners extra leeway, to persuade yourself that you must look a little further ahead.

It may help to consider the momentum. There is no doubt that shares which are moving do gain a momentum, be it up or down. Buying seems to attract buying, and vice versa. If your share has lost momentum, has been stalled in the same narrow price range for two or three months, perhaps a change is on hand. The buyers might be poised to switch to sellers.

Nothing lasts for ever.

Cycles

The stockmarket and the economy always move in cycles. In 1996, we are supposed to believe that the fight against inflation has been won. We are moving into an economy with steady growth and low inflation. Eureka!

Do not believe it. If we are lucky, the period of growth and low inflation may be rather longer than in earlier years. But the cycle will roll around. Good times will be followed by bad, rising markets by falling markets. If you can take your cash out near the top, sit on it, and wait until we get somewhere near the bottom, think how many more investment bargains you can buy.

The notion that you should be permanently invested in shares as a hedge against long-term inflation is nonsense. It may suit the City to have you believe it — if everyone withdrew their cash when the economy looked tricky, the market would collapse completely. And the professional investor could not have that. But as an individual, you can move in and out. That flexibility is worth a fortune. Every day you have your money in the stockmarket, that money is at risk. Do not leave it there through lethargy. Or some muddled notion about long-term investment. Sitting with a loser for the long run has no virtue.

Never be content to sit with a share that is slipping gently lower. Never heed the nonsense which suggests you are not doing badly if your investment has not fallen by as much as the market as a whole. You are not in the market as a whole. If your investment has gone down, you have lost money. That is all that matters.

Reading The Trend

The warning signs, urging you to sell, are often there in the market, if you can read them. Watch how your share behaves against the trend. If it slips on a day when the market is steady, wonder why. If it fails to respond when the market rises strongly, wonder why. If it falls more sharply on a dull day, wonder why.

Someone always knows more than you. He may not tell you it, but the price may give you a clue. You may not know what the insiders are saying. The share price helps tell you what they are doing.

Other Sell Signs

There are other signs. Obviously if the talk should be of an economic slump ahead, and the whole market is slipping, ask yourself whether your company can buck that trend. Beware. If it is a tiddler in the AIM, that is unlikely. AIM and OFEX shares do shrug off short-term blips. Some have such startling growth projections that they may be a special case. But a serious market slump could send the fledgling markets crashing, growth stocks or not.

You can pick up other warning signs by watching the competition. If your favourite is in the hotel trade, and the big names start reporting tougher trading, it may filter down to your share. Sell. Watch allied industries. If house sales slump, estate agents suffer. So do brick-makers, carpet companies, furniture stores.

If one of the more prominent directors — chairman, chief executive, or finance director — leaves for no terribly obvious reason, watch out. There might be bad news to come. Try to discover why he left. It could be a good sign if someone new, with a big reputation, comes in.

If the shares run ahead suddenly on a tip in some newspaper or tip sheet, ask yourself if that provides a selling opportunity. A big rise could push the price ahead of the game, and it might be possible to take a quick profit and buy back a few weeks later if the market settles lower.

When To Stay Away

No matter what the state of the market, there are some shares which move steadily ahead. No matter how grim, a small number have such strong prospects that they buck the trend. But they are few and far between. You might find them in the small market companies, given that many of them are young businesses with great potential. But if you are going to stay aboard when the market in general is in clear decline, you need to be very sure.

Unsaleable Shares

In a falling market, smaller shares can be the hardest hit. They may resist the decline at first. But when they start to slide, they will go down further and faster than the big boys. Worse still, they may become unsaleable. This happened to many tiddlers in the wake of the 1987 crash. Market-makers widened prices, and reduced the number of shares in which they would deal.

Shares where once you could buy and sell 10,000 with a 1p spread between buying and selling prices suddenly became quoted in 1,000 shares on a 2p spread. At times, the market was in a mere 500 on a 5p spread. In effect, many small shares could not be sold. They lost all real value. Indeed, there were times when market-makers would not offer a price for some shares in any size. Be under no illusions. That could well happen in the AIM and OFEX investments, if a serious slump sets in. Do not let it catch you. If in doubt, sell out.

When Times Get Tough

When times get tough in the City, the most unexpected things can happen. The bank or broking house which sponsored your fledgling market issue could decide to close the small company department and give up supporting your share. It could go bust, or be sold off. The receiver or the new owner might decide on a change of tack, selling shares in small companies at any price, simply to clear the books.

If something like that happens — and it happened quite frequently in the late eighties and early nineties — your share could almost disappear. The underlying business might be sound enough. It might go from strength to strength. But if no one is interested in making a market in the shares, keeping the flow of interest and information going, you could be in for a very sticky share price.

There is no way out. In the end, share markets are dominated by profit and loss. If no one can make a profit following the shares which interest you, they will walk away. And you could lose your money.

Never think that the worst cannot happen. The City is a nasty, ruthless place when business is bad and costs need to be cut. Your company may be in the middle of a marvellous five-year plan. That may work. But it is no guarantee against the share price stumbling and falling almost out of sight along the way. If the company is good enough, it may survive — though bad times in the City usually mean bad times in the banks, and an undue readiness to pull in loans and bankrupt the most blameless companies.

Always stay near the exit. Never tell yourself you are in for a five-year run, or a ten-year programme. That might seem sensible if you want to support a growing business. But that is not your business. You are hunting the wilder markets in search of share trading profits, nothing else. You are taking a high risk in the hope of a high return. If the going looks like getting tough — get going. Pull your cash out of shares, and go into something boring, predictable and safe — a building society account, or National Savings. Leave it there until the mood changes. Leave it for years, if necessary. That way, you live to gamble another day.

APPENDIX

The Advisers

The scene is changing all of the time, and it is easy for investment books to remain detached, spouting theory, forgetting the practical. That is not for me. Wherever possible, I try to get down to what might be of greatest value to readers. So, fingers crossed, I have tried to give a glimpse of who might be doing what in the AIM and OFEX. The following section gives a glimpse of some of the more active and interesting sponsors and advisers of companies traded on the fledgling markets. It is by no means comprehensive. New names have been appearing regularly.

Please remember that these comments refer to the past activities of some possible AIM and OFEX advisers. By the time you read this, some may have dropped out, the fortunes of the companies they have floated might have changed completely, and a raft of new advisers might have emerged. The comments are my personal view. If you disagree, and you know better, good luck. You may be right, I may be wrong.

Alongside the advisers, it pays to keep an eye on some of the individual players. There are some you would love to back, others you might hate. There is no such list in this book, but you may find some clues in one of my other books, *How To Make A Killing In The Share Jungle*. Inevitably, some of those comments are out of date, though I update them as new editions appear. It is remarkable, however, how many of the old names crop up again and again — good or not so good.

You should remember that AIM companies require a nominated adviser, who will effectively be responsible to the Stock Exchange for any documents produced by the company which issues shares. That nominated adviser will often be the nominated broker, and may make a market in the shares, and keep in touch with what is happening. Most advisers will be stockbrokers, though some are accountants or corporate finance houses. Obviously, the quality of both adviser and broker is crucial.

OFEX companies will usually have the equivalent of a nominated adviser, but that is not always so. They may effectively be sponsored by a corporate finance boutique which is not subject to Stock Exchange rules. There may not be a stockbroker involved, and the standard of professional advice may not be so high as with AIM companies — though some advisers who are too small to qualify as AIM advisers do work to high standards.

Listed alphabetically, these are among the advisers you may stumble across. As an investor in fledgling market companies, I have supported issues from some of these names, and may have held shares in some of the companies mentioned — or may, indeed, still hold them.

Astaire & Co

A small stockbroking house, Astaire & Co placed shares in Transense Technologies in September 1994, and saw them double quickly. Listed on the OFEX, Transense is involved with Jim Perry, a creative but controversial figure with earlier mixed small company experience. Astaire also acts as broker to an AIM flotation, healthcare group Omnicare. Linked with Tim Aitken, that started well in a narrow market. Watch with care.

S.P. Angel

A small, long-established stockbroking firm, S.P. Angel began sponsoring modest 4.2 flotations in 1993. It has been highly successful with IES Group, the electronic security company, and initially with Advanced Media Group, which is involved in electronic information services, and has survived some problems. Too small to qualify as an AIM sponsor.

Austin Friars Securities

Emerging as an OFEX sponsor, it made a solid show with Famous Pub Company. Controversial background of some of those involved suggest it should be treated with care until it establishes a much longer track record.

Beeson Gregory

One of the best-known small-company specialist brokers, Beeson Gregory has taken a conservative approach to backing AIM listings. It has scored early successes with Active Imaging and restaurant group Ask Central. Good, solid reputation.

Branston & Gothard

A smallish, colourful broking house, Branston & Gothard attracted attention when one of the partners was taken to court on a ridiculous charge over remarks expressing a poor opinion of Maxwell Communications Corporation. The case collapsed. Sponsored Multisofft, a company marketing toilet tissue made in China from cotton waste which soon hit problems behind the scenes, and then hit bigger, more public problems. Not an encouraging example. Approach with caution.

Brown Shipley

Established merchant bank which has seen better days, Brown Shipley has sponsored a series of initially unremarkable issues with a steady performance.

Collins Stewart

A relatively new and lively stockbroking firm, Collins Stewart has sponsored several AIM issues without attracting much attention. Bright reputation.

Dunbar, Boyle & Kingsley

A small broker, Dunbar, Boyle & Kingsley has taken great interest in the AIM area. It floated its own shares on the 4.2 market before getting a bid, and floated Athelney, a small investment trust to specialise in AIM type shares.

Durlacher

A small stockbroking firm rebuilding after a speculative reputation, Durlacher itself is floated on AIM as part of Financial Publications. Attempting to build a presence in multimedia markets. A sometime sponsor on the OFEX market.

Ellis & Partners

A small broker based in Crawley, Sussex, Ellis & Partners sponsored several interesting small company issues before AIM was set up. One of the Ellis directors is Clive Mattock, whose success in promoting small company shares has sometimes raised eyebrows. In 1995 and 1996, after failing to qualify as an

AIM sponsor, the firm emerged as nominated broker to a large number of small companies sponsored by others, usually with success. Ellis has also been behind several small OFEX issues, some more speculative than others. Initial progress has been good. Enterprising, but investors should take a selective approach.

English Trust
English Trust has emerged as an active sponsor of AIM issues, in conjunction with several brokers. Initial results have been mixed, with Internet access provider Easynet (floated with broker Collins Stewart) the biggest disappointment in share price performance.

Gerrard Vivian Gray
An established broking firm, Gerrard Vivian Gray has sponsored some AIM issues which have raised eyebrows by their speculative nature.

Grant Thornton
Grant Thornton is an accounting firm which caused a stir by bringing Gabriel Trust to OFEX. Gabriel has been behind several fledgling market issues, but director David Pearl was associated with small quoted companies which hit problems in the late eighties.

Greig Middleton
A solid broking firm, Greig Middleton has a mixed AIM sponsorship record, marred by poor results from taxi firm Hansom.

Guinness Mahon
A smallish merchant bank with a chequered history since the mid-eighties, Guinness Mahon still suffers from the collapse of several prominent BES issues which it promoted.

Henderson Crosthwaite
A sizeable broker, Henderson Crosthwaite has made a reasonable impact on AIM. The best-known issue has been highly rated speciality stores chain Pet City.

Henry Cooke, Lumsden

One of the best-known regional brokers, originally based in Manchester, Henry Cooke has floated several highly successful technology companies on the main market. Late in 1994, it also floated Memory Corporation, a computer chip company which attracted great excitement, and doubled on the first day of trading. It later moved to AIM, rocketed to 14 times the original issue price, then got caught by the collapse in chip prices and tumbled to three times the issue price.

Henry Cooke has sponsored other exciting hi-tech issues, including car gearbox designer Antonov, alongside such solid and successful issues as Surrey Free Inns and brewers Jennings Brothers. Well worth watching. Took software group Softvision to OFEX in April 1996.

Neill Clerk Capital

Originally becoming known as a sponsor of BES issues, Neill Clerk has become one of the most active AIM sponsors, linking with a variety of brokers. Bio-tech company Stanford Rook has initially been a strong, if controversial performer. Mixed performance may depend on which broker is behind each issue.

Peel Hunt

A lively, relatively new broker, Peel Hunt has established a bright reputation among smaller companies, and has backed some OFEX issues. Initial performance has been uneven.

Raphael Zorn Hunt

A smallish broker, Raphael Zorn Hunt sponsored the flotation of Omnimedia, a company in the CD-ROM business. The shares quickly went to a significant premium, though several of those involved had formerly dealt with the controversial Over-The-Counter securities house Harvard Securities, which failed after attracting great controversy in the eighties. Omnimedia has since been more erratic.

Raphael Zorn has also sponsored several small, highly speculative issues such as Silkbarn and London Fiduciary. High risk.

Rowan Dartington
Smallish AIM sponsor, attracting attention for high profile speculative issues such as South American oil explorer Pan Andean, and Zimbabwe gold explorer African Gold.

St James' Partners
A small corporate finance boutique, St James' Partners does not qualify for AIM sponsorship, but has backed a string of small OFEX issues. Highly speculative, but encouraging early success.

Shore Capital
A smallish broking house in which property giant British Land has a stake, Shore Capital brought the Whitchurch Group meat business and the Furlong Homes housebuilder to the 4.2 market in 1994. CD-ROM maker Multimedia followed. Performance of some of Shore's issues has been disappointing but the presentation is first-class. Sponsorship of Saatchi-backed Megalomedia introduces a livelier element.

Singer & Friedlander
A sizeable merchant bank which owns stockbroker Collins Stewart, Singer & Friedlander raised eyebrows over sponsorship of controversial Internet and media company Firecrest, although both subsequently resigned as advisers.

Smith & Williamson
Sponsored several solid BES issues, though not all were without problems. Good, conservative reputation.

Charles Stanley
An established broking firm, Charles Stanley has sponsored several reasonably successful issues.

Teather & Greenwood
Another established smallish broker, Teather & Greenwood supported the 4.2 listing for Moorepay Group, which supplies packaged payroll services, with plans to go for a full listing. It has also acted for recruitment agency Abacus Recruitment, and Pavilion Books, the publishing company whose founders

include Sir Tim Rice and Michael Parkinson. A major question mark looms with involvement in the offer by Aussie group Media Technology Corporation for Faxcast Broadcast Corporation, which is headed by former bankrupt and highly controversial financier Herbert Towning. Subsequent issues have looked solid and sensible.

Williams de Broe

A substantial private client broker, Williams de Broe has been a prominent 4.2 sponsor. It floated the roller-coaster price mover Tracker Network, and followed late in 1994 with Surface Electronics, a printed circuit board testing and production company, and Biotal, a small established company developing and applying commercial applications for bioscience. Other issues include Unimed, a company seeking to develop pharmaceutical products linked with Trinity College, Dublin.

It is behind SCS Satellite Communications which was suspended in 1996 after hitting problems. That is a nasty blot on the broker's reputation.

Words Of Warning

Playing small company shares is a high-risk business. Do not get sucked in too deep. Once your name starts appearing on share registers, or as a subscriber to tip sheets, you may receive all manner of investment propositions through the post.

Never take up any of them up without first seeking advice.

Never part with a penny if you are approached by telephone. The friendly fellow who wants to do you a favour only wants your money.

Never be tempted into any form of investment in commodities, futures, options or overseas shares. You will lose in the end.

Never sign any agreement saying you understand the risks unless you really do understand how the scheme works, and what those risks may be.

Never trust the so-called professional who answers your queries with assurances that he knows how it is done, you can leave it to him. He will end up with your money.

The instant your share punting starts to worry you, pull out. Once investment ceases to be fun, forget it.

If you do have problems, and if you are worried about some dodgy scheme or share pusher, by all means telephone me or write to me at the *Daily Mail.* I take such things very seriously. Even if I cannot help you, I may be able to help others escape the trap. Please, though, accept my apologies in advance if I do not write back. I always intend to, but often the pressure of work is such that I do not get round to it. But I always take notice of letters.

Good luck.

MICHAEL WALTERS

INDEX

ALSO AVAILABLE FROM RUSHMERE WYNNE

HOW TO MAKE A KILLING IN PENNY SHARES
by Michael Walters
(Price £9.99 Paperback)
ISBN 0 948035 20 X

The author has drawn on his thirty years' experience as a financial journalist to produce this definitive guide to probably the most undersub-
scribed area of the stockmarket. This updated edition of his best-selling
book gives a vital insight into the pitfalls and the potential of penny shares,
where fortune and good judgement can turn a few hundred pounds into
thousands.

HOW TO MAKE A KILLING IN THE SHARE JUNGLE
by Michael Walters
(Price £14.99 Paperback)
ISBN 0 948035 19 6

The most comprehensive guide yet to the ups, downs, thrills and spills of
stockmarket investment. In his inimitably straightforward and punchy
style, Michael Walters reveals his recipe for reaping maximum profits
from your investments. He shows how to back the winners without sacrificing your shirt and — crucially — how to know when the party's over
and it's time to sell. Whether you are an absolute beginner or a seasoned
investor, this book will help you. It's a jungle out there.

Rushmere Wynne
are publishers of finance, investment and management books
If you would like a copy of our current catalogue

Please write to:

Rushmere Wynne
4-5 Harmill
Grovebury Road
Leighton Buzzard
Bedfordshire
LU7 8FF

or fax: 01525 852037   or phone: 01525 853726